THE TRUTH ABOUT THE AMERICAN PIT BULL TERRIER

TS-142

Title page: **American Pit Bull Terrier owned by Lynn Fergeson, photographed by Isabelle Français.**

Distributed in the UNITED STATES by T.F.H. Publications, Inc., One T.F.H. Plaza, Neptune City, NJ 07753; in CANADA to the Pet Trade by H & L Pet Supplies Inc., 27 Kingston Crescent, Kitchener, Ontario N2B 2T6; Rolf C. Hagen Ltd., 3225 Sartelon Street, Montreal 382 Quebec; in CANADA to the Book Trade by Macmillan of Canada (A Division of Canada Publishing Corporation), 164 Commander Boulevard, Agincourt, Ontario M1S 3C7; in ENGLAND by T.F.H. Publications, The Spinney, Parklands, Portsmouth PO7 6AR; in AUSTRALIA AND THE SOUTH PACIFIC by T.F.H. (Australia) Pty. Ltd., Box 149, Brookvale 2100 N.S.W., Australia; in NEW ZEALAND by Ross Haines & Son, Ltd., 82 D Elizabeth Knox Place, Panmure, Auckland, New Zealand; in the PHILIP-PINES by Bio-Research, 5 Lippay Street, San Lorenzo Village, Makati Rizal; in SOUTH AFRICA by Multipet Pty. Ltd., Box 235 New Germany, South Africa 3620. Published by T.F.H. Publications, Inc. Manufactured in the United States of America by T.F.H. Publications, Inc.

The Truth About The American Pit Bull Terrier

by
Richard F. Stratton

American Pit Bull adult and pups owned by Pet Barbers/Eric Rosenstein. Photo by Isabelle Français.

Contents

*This book is dedicated to my three sisters
—Louise, Claudia, and Marie—
who had to endure an   older
—and wiser!—
brother.*

Opposite: Sandy Musgrove and Susie,
an inbred daughter of Heinzl's
Cowboy Bob.

Introduction

"Be kind. Because everyone is fighting his own battle."
AUTHOR UNKNOWN

This book is my fourth on the American Pit Bull Terrier. The reader may wonder how I could possibly write four books on one breed of dog. After all, an old friend once said when he heard (many years ago) that I was going to do a *second* book, "What in the world are you going to write about? You've already covered *everything* in the first book!"

However, the American Pit Bull Terrier or "Bulldog," as he is more likely to be called by those who know him best, is not merely another breed of dog. I could write *volumes* about him! And I would never run out of something new to discourse upon, to wonder at, or simply to raise for debate or discussion among the fancy. You will see as you read these pages that I am at once hardpressed to get in everything that I want to say: I am concerned that readers really understand what I'm saying; yet, I do not want to belabor a point; and, I am impatient with those who know nothing about the breed but are all too willing to attack it. In other words, I've developed an emotional commitment to a breed of dog. I get depressed if I read some ill-begotten press about it; and my spirits are raised on those rare occasions when the breed is somehow shown as it really is—a truly wonderful and remarkable animal.

Just the other day, for example, I took Hoover, one of my kennel dogs,

dogs, to the veterinarian for a look at a swollen paw. It was, as I suspected, merely an insect bite; but the point is that I had to take him to a new veterinarian, as my regular was out of town, and the new one—much to my delight!—simply could not stop extolling upon the virtues of the dog. He rested his hand on Hoover's head in a frank expression of admiration and said, "It is a pleasure to treat a dog such as this." I could tell by his entire demeanor that he really meant it, and it made me feel as proud as though the dog were my son and had received a sincere and rare type of compliment.

It is not without a certain amount of chagrin that I confide such an attachment to a breed of dog—even if it is not just another breed. Although the breed is truly unique and has detractors who threaten its very existence, surely there are causes which are more worthy of a man's attention. As a matter of fact, I have other causes, too. And it so happens that, although I am a science teacher by trade, I have had the opportunity to write political commentary for newspapers. Although I enjoy being paid to pontificate, I somehow do not feel that such writings are more

Webb's Brus Balboa indulging in the last refuge of scoundrels. Owner, Danny Webb.

Behne's Red Dawn on fish watch.

important than those I have written about the good old American Pit Bull Terrier.

Nevertheless, it was not without a certain amount of trepidation that I first began to write about the breed. I knew that my reputation might be harmed, as I would be accused of condoning dog-fighting, and such a condemnation without debate could be the kiss of death for many endeavors in an uncertain future. And, sure enough, such did indeed prove to be the case. But, even anticipating that, I plunged ahead, as I had decided that a cause was important to the meaning of life, and the more hopeless a cause was and the less gratification achieved from it, the more noble and unselfish would be my motives.

But knowing something and actually experiencing it are two different things, and there were times when I was quite willing to kick my noble and unselfish *derriere* up the road for a good long way. Fortunately, such times didn't last forever. Now I receive unanticipated rewards for all this writing about such a controversial animal. Famous football players, who happen to be devotees of the APBT breed, have sought me out for *my* autograph! I have even had some of them visit my house to see my dogs. This has been enjoyable for me, as I am a football fan of sorts. To this gratification has

Slater's and Chevez's Captain Crunch. Owner, Butch Slater. *Opposite:* **Mims's Femme Boots Koty is down from the renowned Tramp's Red Boy. Owner, Debbie Smollich.**

been added the physicians and scientists I have met, who also happen to be devotees of the dog. Many of them I most assuredly would not have met if it had not been for my writings on the breed.

A particular redemption has been that humane agents (whom I often berated in the past as "humaniacs," a term that was adopted by the newspapers) have sought me out for advice, or at least for my opinion, about different aspects of the breed or legislation involving it. It is my hope that, since animal welfare people—some of them, at least—can give credence to what I have said, the general public will realize that what follows is, in my opinion, the absolute truth about the American Pit Bull Terrier.

Above: A Pit Bull enjoys working a hide or a tire. *Opposite:* Hammonds's Andy L, the sire of several good pit dogs such as Rufin, Red Doodle, and Roberto.

A Bulldog owned by Thomas Scanlan. *Opposite:* **Bulldogs on guard duty.**

The Truth About the American Pit Bull Terrier

> *"My way of joking is to tell the truth. It's the funniest joke in the world."*
> GEORGE BERNARD SHAW

If I were to tell you that I acquired a Border Collie for a pet, you might not know what the dog was, but you wouldn't be horrified—particularly after I had explained that the breed was used for herding sheep. If, on the other hand, I were to inform you that I had just obtained a Pit Bull puppy, you *would* be horrified. Not being immune to the media blitz, you would have it set in your mind that this was truly a dangerous animal, roughly equivalent to a baby rattlesnake. The pup would grow to be dangerous and was bound eventually to turn on me and to devour my children in the bargain. Having done all this, the dog quite likely would escape my premises and proceed to destroy the city.

But all this is nonsense, and I have said that I would tell the truth. All right, this is the truth: The Border Collie would be much more likely to bite my children or me than the Pit Bull! And please let me make it clear that I am personally a great admirer of the Border Collie; however, I am also willing to be honest about that breed, and its members are a little nippy— especially with strangers. The point is that *any* breed comes off second to the Pit Bull in terms of stable disposition with people. How ironic it is that this most gentle of breeds has become a household word as the incarnation of savagery! Of all dogs, this breed is most likely to elicit the comment, "Why on earth do you want

Juli is a dog in Norway, so her name is pronounced "you-lee."

to keep a dog like that?" Let me now describe what the dog is really like.

First, let me drop the term "Pit Bull." I have used it only because that is how this dog is known to the general public. Other breeds also get thrown into this category, so it is a term I prefer not to use. Henceforth, I'll refer to the American Pit Bull Terrier breed as "Bulldog," because that is how he is known by those who know him best. Occasionally I'll use

John Maranghi's Dharma, a daughter of Hoover and Tar.

the formal name or the initials APBT.

Anyway, a typical Bulldog can be shamefully mistreated without biting anyone. He will take maulings from young children and thrive upon it. He likes rough play, as long as he knows it is play, and is tireless in his indulgence. One of the most uniform characteristics of the breed is the great love for play. The capacity for play is often cited as an indication of a species' intelligence. I agree with that idea, but it is also a manifestation of an enthusiasm for life. Bulldogs have a bountiful supply of such enthusiasm, and everything can become a plaything for them. For kennel dogs, it can be the feed pan or rocks that are utilized as objects of play. House dogs immediately take to a ball or a frisbee or anything else you would like to have them use. And, since Bulldogs so readily settle on what is to be a toy and what isn't, destruction of other property is usually not a problem. Because he comes so often to mind as I describe

Right: Kelly Weldon with daughter Amber and dog Jake.
Below: Chico, a champion tree climber, as so many Bulldogs are.

Left: Blaze, a one-time winner, is down from Rascal Jr. and Chinaman.
Below: Trouble.

Opposite: Carroll's Breen leaping for a stick.

Boozer, the Strattons' house dog.

the nature of the Bulldog and because he lies at my feet this very minute as I write, let me describe my own house dog, Boozer, and some of my experiences with him.

Boozer is the son of Burton's Dillinger, a dog that stopped what was thought to be an unbeatable pit dog in a roll and later lost a match in a little over two hours against a dog named Weasil. Dillinger lost the match when his handler picked him up to save his life. There had been no turns in the contest. Dillinger's mother was Reddick's Chigger, the dam of the famous Simon. Boozer's mother was by Burton's Spade (a red dog, believe it or not, and a great pit dog) and out of Delta Dawn. The reason for citing Boozer's immediate ancestors is for the reader to understand clearly that Boozer is from straight pit stock.

From the time Boozer came into the house as a young pup, he never once soiled the carpet in any way.

Amber Weldon and Jake.

He house-trained himself from the start. His disposition is unbelievably mellow and always has been. I have two sons attending college who are still living at home, and they love to show off to their horrified friends how vicious this Bulldog is. They will take him down and sit on him, holding him with handgrips on each side of his neck. Boozer will roar with mock, but convincing, fury. An onlooker, brainwashed by the reputation of the breed or not, is convinced that my son is a "goner" once he turns loose this canine gone mad. No such thing, of course, as it is all part of the game. Upon being turned loose, Boozer resumes silent play. What's more, although my sons can be rough with him, he still treats them as though they were babies, never even mouthing them and never putting a scratch on them.

Although I have always maintained that Boozer was dumb for a Bulldog, my sons stoutly defend him and have taught him a number of parlor tricks. He performs them adroitly with an artful clumsiness—well enough that he is a favorite of all visitors. His own favorites seem mainly to be girls, so perhaps he is not as dumb as I thought! Actually, he probably prefers girls simply because they pet him and make more over him than the boys and men that visit here. Being petted and loved is something upon which he thrives, and, like so many Bulldogs, he can actually grin when   receiving nearly all the attention he craves.

Like so many dogs, Boozer enjoys going for an outing of any kind. If I believed in E.S.P., I would believe that Boozer has it, as he has an uncanny ability to know when someone is going out—someplace where he might be invited. We have even resorted to spelling at times to deceive him—all to no avail!

Part of what makes Boozer such

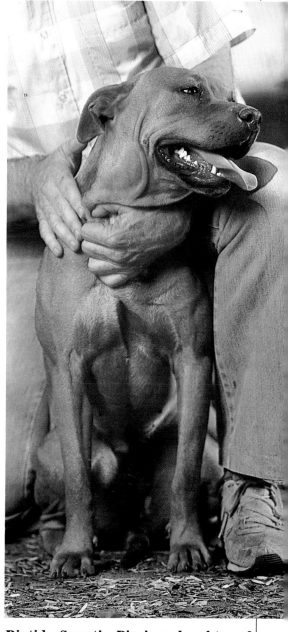

Riptide Sweetie Pie is a daughter of Hoover and a granddaughter of Grand Champion Hope. Owner, Dick Stratton.

Nightman's Diesel is a son of Grand Champion Red John and a grandson of the great Jeep dog. Owner, Ed Laddomada.

good company and so much fun to have around is his expressiveness. And that goes beyond his facial expressions as, amazing as they are, they are limited by the fact that he is, after all, a dog. He makes sounds that, while not words, still communicate his feelings and his needs nearly as well. That is not to say that he is a noisy animal, as, like nearly all Bulldogs, he rarely barks. His communicative sounds are plaintive, amusing, and instructive, but they are never obnoxious.

Because of his appearance, Boozer terrorizes most strangers; so when newcomers come to call, he is restricted to the back of the house until I've been able to explain Boozer to the persons involved and ascertain that they would not be made uncomfortable by him. The opinion has been almost unanimously expressed that Boozer is the most polite dog that has ever

been seen and is utterly charming in every way. Surely not all of this is an attempt to flatter his owners.

Boozer can be trusted with our house cat and with all other cats, too. With strange dogs he is friendly but unafraid. Even though he is much smaller than many of the dogs he meets, he seems to intimidate them somehow; and the other dog's tail is usually down as noses are sniffed. Boozer doesn't take advantage of his intimidating effect—whatever it is— and no dog has ever attacked him. Obviously, we have kept him from confronting other Bulldog males, as he quite likely would be attacked then, and we don't wish him to gain an appetite for fighting.

In short, then, Boozer comes pretty close to being the perfect house dog. Even though he has his breed's typical mellow disposition with people, his appearance at sixty pounds serves to make him an

Although Bulldogs can be friends forever, these tug of war games call for a little supervision.

Above: Gina at four months. **Left:** Julie Romero with Squeezer out of Bullyson bloodlines.

Opposite: Emmerts's Tugger.

excellent watch dog—even though he doesn't bark. He will still be there to greet a potential burglar, and few would enter upon seeing him. Whether he would actually attack an intruder or not is something I don't know, but the breed is known for its good judgment about when to go into action. In any case, it is only of academic interest, as just being here and watchful seems to serve the purpose, for his appearance and the breed's reputation ensures that burglars are extremely unlikely to strike here.

He is intelligent and entertaining—not to mention endearing—and he has a short, clean coat that makes him a clean and basically odorless house pet. He is game for any type of outing or play, so he is an excellent companion for those of us who are into physically demanding endeavors, such as jogging or hiking. The boys often take him on hiking or skiing excursions, and he has a riotously good time without causing any problems. It is hard to keep from repeating that the dog is an ideal pet in every way. Of course, some people might prefer that he be smaller, and that's just it! Bulldogs come in all sizes, so you can have one that peaks at only thirty pounds and still have a delightful animal that is all dog and, most assuredly, no sissy!

The question is, "How typical is Boozer?" Well, I wouldn't have utilized him as an example if he were not typical of the breed in nearly every respect. Many Bulldogs, however, are going to develop an urge to fight even if confrontations with other dogs are avoided. About 40% of them will kill strange cats,

and those that are inclined to go after cats will also most likely attack bigger game, from cattle to mountain lions. To be truthful, a good percentage of Bulldogs will be a hazard to all other dogs, and many will be dangerous to have around livestock. In fact, they would even be a danger to big Texas longhorn steers. Such dogs must simply be kept on a leash, as is required by law in most cities and states; and we even keep Boozer on a lead when he is taken out, even though the only necessity is compliance with the city's ordinance.

Let me emphasize, though, that Boozer's easygoing attitude with other dogs doesn't make him a freak within the breed. Many are that way—including some renowned pit dogs. Jimmy Boots is one example that springs immediately to mind. A world-famous and bone-crushing pit dog, Jimmy Boots was raised as a family dog and left other dogs alone—unless they made the terrible mistake of attacking him. He was also an intelligent animal that had been trained to do tricks. One of the more ribald ones being that when he was asked what the girls in Laramie (a town noted for its houses of prostitution) did, he would roll over on his back with his legs spread.

In summary, the breed is an ideal house pet; it is intelligent, with a convenient short coat, and an absolutely flawless disposition with people. However, many hundreds of years as first a hunter and later as a fighter have made the breed the most formidable of dogs. It is this characteristic, together with other circumstances, that has created the awesome reputation.

I have extolled the virtues of the breed not because I want it to become popular. It is too popular now—that is part of the problem. The reason I am so laudatory about the animal is, first of all, he is deserving of any praise I, or anyone else, might bestow upon him. He merits praise and, most assuredly, commands respect. A second reason is that the breed is under siege. This is the only breed of which I am aware that has ever been outlawed specifically from any municipality. This fact not only frightens me, it angers me greatly, for the injustice of it all can only be known by those who know the breed as it really is— by those who know the *truth* about the American Pit Bull Terrier.

Chance Dancing Goldie is a much admired bitch.

Right: Here Rose's Red Cole places first at a California dog show. *Below:* This is the predominant disposition of Pit Bulls with children—not the aberrations that have been featured in the media.

Gary and Linda Emmerts go trick or treating with their Bulldog Tugger.

Right: American Pit Bull Terrier owned by Charles M. Kopenhafer. *Below:* Champion Butch is a son of Champion Saloon.

Above: Kolohe at one year of age with his favorite toy, a full-sized tire. *Opposite:* Under proposed anti-Pit Bull legislation, this puppy would be taken from these young people.

Headline Mentality

> *"Credulous acceptance of baloney can lose you money; that's what P.T. Barnum meant when he said, 'There's a sucker born every minute.' But it can be much more dangerous than that, and when governments and societies lose the capacity for critical thinking, the results can be catastrophic"*
>
> CARL SAGAN

The catastrophe in this particular instance is the outlawing of a breed. Such events have taken place in many communities, even at times including other breeds in the ordinance. To be fair, the ordinances usually don't simply outlaw breeds, but the effect is the same if an inordinate amount of insurance is required and the insurance companies will not grant insurance. Other laws prescribe a leash (of a specified length) and a muzzle to be utilized when walking a specific breed.

The strategy of anti-dog groups is clear. They have found a weak spot in the dog world in that the American Pit Bull Terrier is perceived as such a dangerous animal. If they can outlaw this one breed, it will set the precedent for others. In fact, as I said, other breeds have already been included. But the question is: "How did the APBT ever attain such a horrendous reputation and thus become vulnerable?" It is not a question for which there is an easy answer.

One of the problems is that the history of the breed evokes an automatic image of a fierce creature. Ancient artwork shows dogs that look just like modern APBTs being used as hunting dogs (that is, hunting dogs in the ancient sense, dogs that go in and help kill the prey). Later the identical dogs were used by butchers to help them capture a bull in the yard that they wanted to slaughter. Bullbaiting probably developed as a sport that was an outgrowth of this activity. In any case, it was this activity that gave the breed the name "Bulldog." (They were also known in other times and other lands as "bull biters" and "bear biters.")

Since the modern English (or show) Bulldog is no longer able to hunt wild boar or catch a bull by the nose and subdue it, and the modern American Pit Bull is still capable of exactly those things, most APBT fanciers are inclined to think that it is their breed that is the purest form

Left: **Bruiser, a 47-pound dog.**

Opposite: **Sir Winston hanging from a training sleeve.**

of the real, old-time Bulldog; hence, the casual name for him that has been retained throughout the ages.

The public, however, is not aware of the hunting history of the breed, but they are all too cognizant of the reputation of the breed as a pit fighter. To people who don't give a whole lot of deep thought to the subject, it seems only natural that a fighting dog must be aggressive toward people, too. It is an automatic assumption of sorts, and people can't be blamed for making it.

The truth is, though, that there has been a selective process going on for centuries. It only stands to reason, for example, that the ancient hunters would kill any dog that

STB and Hall's Champion Sugar is a four-time winner and a daughter of Wood's Snooty.

turned on them—especially if it tried to dispute with the humans over the kill.

Later—no one knows when—the breed became the dog of preference for canine-fighting contests. The dogs were used as fighters because of the breed's endurance, tolerance to pain, agility, and gameness. Gameness means the perseverance of the dog regardless of circumstances. Many of these traits no doubt originated in the breed's development as a "kill dog" in the hunt. In dog-fighting contests, however, the dogs were *not* just thrown into a cage and allowed to fight inside. A referee and two handlers were with them during the entire period. The dogs were often picked up and ministered to. For that reason, dogs that were inclined to bite, out of pain or savagery, were culled and, thus, not allowed to pass on such a trait.

The natural inclination is to think that if a dog is a killer of other animals, it certainly must be of an unreliable disposition with people. But think of retrievers. They have excellent dispositions with humans even though they have strong instincts to go after birds. The same is true of Redbone Coonhounds, which are used for tracking and attacking everything from raccoons to bears; yet, they have an outstanding disposition with humans simply because the historical breeders were completely intolerant of "people-mean" dogs.

Why all the hullabaloo in the media then? I was puzzled by the phenomenon myself, for I have never once owned a Bulldog that would bite anyone.

For whatever reason, the breed has undergone explosive popularity in the past twelve years. Unfortunately, the dogs seem to appeal to certain macho types who

Above: **Pat with Kitty, Richard with Honey, and Patricia with Tucker demonstrate that Bulldogs aren't necessarily enemies.** *Below:* **Behne's Clyde looking impressively sinewy.**

Slater's Samson Lee, a weight-pull ace. Owner, Butch Slater.

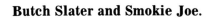

Butch Slater and Smokie Joe.

are inclined to be irresponsible and who are boastful about how formidable and vicious their charges are. This particular group of people may be breeding dogs that are more "people-mean" than is normal of the breed.

Things seem to have gained an impetus of their own in the news media. A Pit Bull bite is more likely to make the news than a bite from any other breed. Even bites that aren't verified Pit Bull bites often get reported if suspected as such. Many mixed-breed incidents certainly are reported as though the dogs are pure Pit Bulls. (I have lapsed back into the "Pit Bull" terminology, because that is what the media uses.) A television news broadcast *featured* a story recently about an accidental fight between a Chow and a Pit Bull. Even the *San Diego Tribune* a couple of years back had a front-page story about a *barking* Pit Bull. While it is not typical of the *Tribune* to be so cavalier about its news placement, neither is it typical of Pit Bulls to be barkers. It is also not typical of them to be a threat to any humans.

I'm not saying that there have been *no* attacks by Pit Bulls upon people. Certainly there have been. But these are rare aberrations of the breed. If there is a dog bite and there is any room for doubt, the Pit Bull will get the blame.

Nearly every single breed has been involved in attacks on humans. About twelve years ago, three Pekingese mobbed and killed an infant. But, of course, most of the serious attacks are by large breeds for the simple reason that they are more capable of inflicting damage.

Mrs. Lehman and Star.

STB's Frankie is a double-bred Snooty dog.

The American Pit Bull Terrier is not a big dog, normally weighing between thirty and sixty pounds. However, there is no denying that he is capable of inflicting tremendous damage. The point is that he is much less likely to do so than breeds you've never even heard of.

Yes, he is a danger to other dogs—in spite of all his sweetness with humans. Some individuals also could be a danger to livestock—including large, longhorn steers. The law holds anyone accountable for the damage his dog does. For that reason, owning a Pit Bull is not a responsibility to be taken lightly. But it is not so difficult to keep a dog confined or on a leash, as is required by law for all breeds. For those of us who consider this most unjustly reviled breed as

the best of dogs, it is worth the inconvenience.

So we see that the infamy of the Pit Bull has been brought about by a number of complex and varied causes. First, of course, is the opportunism of the anti-dog factions. Second is the propensity of the news media to gravitate toward any alleged Pit Bull story and to sensationalize it as much as possible. As one young journalist told me, "Pit Bulls are a 'sexy topic' right now." By that, she meant that Pit Bulls were a hot topic, one that would sell newspapers and fill up sensationalistic space when the murderers and rapists were resting. Third is a natural tendency for the public automatically to think the worst of the breed because they know of it as a fighting dog. Fourth is another natural tendency of the public to peruse the headlines and to do so with absolutely no critical thinking involved. We all do it to a degree; it depends, I suppose, to a certain extent upon how interested we are in the subject involved.

The truth is that we should all be more skeptical and inquiring about everything that we read (or, even more so, about what we see and hear in the news media). I don't know who first used the term "headline mentality," but it is a wonderfully descriptive term for the type of intellect that does absolutely no probing, no independent or critical thinking, and simply swallows the whole "circus" that is presented by the news media. It is a little depressing to observe humans whose strong opinions have simply been programmed into them by whatever news they've been exposed to.

Don't get me wrong. I am not of the opinion that there is a dark plot by news people to vilify the Pit Bull. But reporters are human, and they know what sells newspapers and makes their bosses happy. Besides, they have many stories to cover. Hence, if there is a reaction to what they have written, it has to be an awfully big one for them to go back and re-examine it, for they are already on another story. So, no, I'm not blaming reporters, but I'm not blind to the fact that most news stories have inaccuracies in them. In news stories not involving the dogs about which I have been privy to the facts, the stories in the papers were unbelievably jumbled—or just plain false. Often I could trace back events to see why the stories came out the way they did. Most of the time, it was simply honest mistakes by reporters, with no malice intended.

Still, we have to keep in mind that we must keep a skeptical attitude about all stories—including those that appear in the news. Failure to do so will leave us with a very distorted view of the world. And only Bulldog people can fully appreciate how badly the image their breed has been injured. Unfortunately, this distorted view of the Pit Bull has led to some dangerous consequences.

These girls are having fun getting ready to show their Bulldogs.

Above: Nancy Benson with her dog, the great Champion Bobby McGee. *Opposite:* Gary Hammonds with his great Rufus dog.

Above: Champion Gideon is a pit dog whose photo hangs in a popular restaurant. *Opposite:* STB's Dylan is a two-time winner and a son of Champion Peterbilt.

Under Siege

> *"I have made but one prayer to God, a very short one: 'Oh Lord, make my enemies ridiculous.' And God granted it."*
>
> VOLTAIRE

Surely no other breed of dog in history has become so infamous. And how ironic it is for such little cause. A breed that some fifteen years ago was nearly unknown is now a household word. What other breed, for example, has been featured in editorial cartoons? Three such cartoons immediately come to mind, and although the presumptions behind them are not funny, I couldn't help a bemused smile when I saw them. One showed a dog carrying a human body into the house by the feet. The lady of the house, observing this, comments to her husband who is occupied in the other room reading the paper, "Harold, remember when we got rid of the Retriever because he kept bringing us all the neighbor's papers and we got a Pit Bull instead?"

Another cartoon that particularly amused me followed upon certain municipalities in California outlawing the Pit Bull, and it showed a Pit Bull in a line-up with a bunch of thugs—other wanted criminals!

Austin's Junior and a camera-shy youngster.

A third showed a bunch of terrorists, drawn to make them look like the most violent of people, with beards and tattoos, and guns, knives, and grenades in their belts, reading a newspaper that was reporting "two more Pit Bull attacks." One of them is saying, "Those dogs scare the fool out of me!"

What has happened is that, because of all the news stories about Pit Bull attacks, there has been a press for ordinances in various parts of the country to prohibit ownership of Pit Bulls and sometimes of "concomitant breeds." The very first ordinance in a large city was in Hollywood, Florida, and that one was overturned by a court as being unconstitutionally discriminating to a specific group of dog owners. Some of the communities have passed the ordinances knowing full well that such a ruling was made. In many cases, it was in such small municipalities that they thought, perhaps, that their ordinance would not be challenged and ruled upon. Unfortunately, the egos of the city councils in the small towns are often even greater than those of their counterparts in large cities, and they aren't about to let anyone tell them what to do. Of course, they knew nothing about the breed that they were legislating against.

The reaction of the general dog community to all this has generally been one of support, I am happy to say, for the other dog owners know that it will set a dangerous precedent for them. Most articles appearing in general dog publications have been against the laws, and the American Dog Owners' Association began legal proceedings

Boudreaux-bloodline pups enchanting a straw-hatted gent. Owner, Jeff Fontenot.

to overturn all the ordinances.

One article by a couple of veterinarians, who obviously had not learned the power of critical thinking, did appear in *Dog World* and was entitled, "Are Pit Bulls Giving Good Dogs a Bad Name?" It attempted to show that the number of bites per Pit Bull was of a greater percentage than it should be. However, the article utilized a faulty data base and some unwarranted assumptions. It should be noted that *most* veterinarians are the first to praise Bulldogs because they are so easy to work on, as they are such cooperative patients.

Such faith do most members of the Bulldog fancy have in the reliable disposition of the breed that most of us consider the reports of *any* attack with a very suspicious eye. The suspicion is well founded in many cases, as the attacks are often by mixed breeds—often with no Bulldog blood in them at all.

Hopefully this Bulldog will be around to see many more Christmases—if the headline hunters don't have their way.

Above: **Kung Fu King on springpole.** *Opposite:* **Hammonds's Little Selma Two will spot an intriguing object a mile off in the distance and stand like this for hours at a time.**

Heinzl's Bozo, a grandson of Heinzl's Chile.

To help illustrate that most so-called Pit Bull attacks are cases of mistaken identity, Al Stone, a Los Angeles policeman-turned-attorney, compiled an identification book of sorts that contained pictures of all the common breeds and of the Bulldog, too. In the cases he was able to investigate (on his own time), all of them were other breeds. In some cases crossbreeds might have been involved, but he discovered that most people were all too eager to say "Pit Bull" when they weren't sure what dog it was. After all, those were the dogs that they had been hearing so much about as being dangerous, weren't they? So, in effect, much of the population had been programmed to cry "Pit Bull" over any dog bite. "Pit Bull" has replaced "mad dog" as the cry of hysteria.

Nevertheless, one morning I heard a report that I knew was a *bona fide* Pit Bull attack. The report was of a dog killing a baby. The story said that the father of the child was mowing his lawn with a power mower, and his Pit Bull kept trying to attack the mower. He placed the dog inside the house with the baby and proceeded to finish mowing the lawn, with the dog all the while railing at the mower through the window. When he re-entered the

***Opposite:* Joe Graham riding his father's great tree-climbing dog Tiger.**

house he was horrified to find the baby's dead and terribly mangled body.

I was heartsick, for I knew that such a scenario was well within the behavior of a Bulldog. Let me explain. I know that it was not uncommon for a Bulldog to want to attack a power mower. (Many react the same way to other equipment— a predator, pure and simple; and he may not recognize the baby as human. After all, an infant looks considerably different from us; it makes strange noises and is down on all fours. For that reason, the percentage of fatalities from dog attacks is very largely comprised of infants. And for that reason, I will not accept the name "baby killer"

Above: **Reid's Billy is a two-time winner.** *Opposite:* **Joe Graham's Buck was the first Bulldog to undergo obedience and protection training in the United Kingdom.**

including, in the old days, steam locomotives!) I also know that if the dog is grown and the baby is newborn, the dog has not been raised with the baby. Consequently, he very likely would not recognize it as human and it could be attacked— especially with the excited state that he was in.

Let me hasten to add that many dog experts have suggested extreme caution about large powerful dogs around babies. The potential problem is that any dog is by nature for the Bulldog unless the caller includes Collies, German Shepherds, Labradors, and humans, too, for they all kill a larger number of babies than the Bulldog.

Anyway, after that first real Bulldog attack, there eventually came others. The reason was that the breed was increasing rapidly in population. Since the breed was not AKC-registered, the results didn't show up in that way. And since the appeal of the breed was especially strong for those people in the lower

Left: **Nick's Brewzer with a pure Manx cat.**

Opposite: **Mims's Hard Jack is by Mims's Pilot out of Clemens's Midnight.**

socio-economic structure, the breed didn't really show up in licensing either. Even with those in the "upper levels," many owners didn't license their dogs under the name "Pit Bull" as a matter of principle, for many of them knew that many local humane agencies include in their "dog-fighter" files all owners of Pit Bulls. And, of course, Pit Bull owners want to keep their options open in case the breed is ever outlawed. (Although I fight hard against it, I really do consider that a dim possibility.) The point is, with the breed so numerous, the potential for problems is increased exponentially. When you throw in the concept that a great percentage of their numbers are in the hands of irresponsible people who know nothing about the breed, the potential for bad press looms even greater.

A recent article in *Dog World* tells of a paramedic's experiences in Harlem. In the article the author states that the most popular breed in Harlem was the Pit Bull. (And I myself have noticed that the breed is truly incredibly popular in lower income neighborhoods that I have visited across the country.) He quotes some of the owners as talking about crossing the dogs with other breeds. Now, crossing a Bulldog with another breed can be a formula for trouble. For if the breed is crossed with even mildly aggressive breeds, such as the Boxer or German Shepherd, the offspring are likely to have the people-aggressive tendencies of the other breed coupled with the intensity and power of the Pit Bull.

A pit-dog man from the East took a job reading meters for a while to supplement the income from his dairy farm during a tough financial year. He noticed that his fellow meter readers were especially wary of Pit Bulls. He tried to tell them how wrong they were, but he discovered for himself that there actually were some out there that *were* people-mean. It is difficult to convey just how shocking this discovery was to a lifetime Bulldog devotee.

Now this doesn't mean that the breed has been ruined. It simply means that, whereas the breed before had almost no people-mean dogs, now there *are* some—just like other breeds! An important point here is that it is the *pit* stock which has the dogs with the *reliable*

disposition with humans; and it is the *pet* stock that is producing the people-mean dogs. This fact is in sharp contrast to the statements in an article by an animal welfare activist, in which she states that dog fighting is not just an animal rights issue but is producing animals that are a threat to humans. It is a clever ploy and perhaps even sincere, but it is totally without merit. For pit-dog men are unimpressed by people-mean dogs, and they routinely cull them.

So, at worst, we have a breed that has degenerated to the level of other breeds in terms of people-meanness; and even that situation is so only if we count in the non-pit stock. Accepting this situation, it seems to me ludicrous for writers such as Dr. Michael Fox, a veterinarian and author of a number of books, to condemn as vicious, in his newspaper column, all Pit Bulls, including American Staffordshire Terriers. According to him, if he wanted such a breed he would send back to England for it (meanwhile, England is importing APBTs from the United States!). I have enjoyed, to a degree, Fox's books on the wolf

Ironman's Blue is a descendant of Peterbilt and Petronellis's Fox.

Pollard's Mike at 60 pounds is an example of the rarer large Pit Bull.

and other wild canids. However, his remarks about the Pit Bull not only show a lack of critical thinking but show poor judgment in making comments about something of which he is obviously woefully ignorant.

Unfortunately, misinformation and ignorant writings can affect the public; and the public, in turn, affects the politicians. Hence, we find the battle lines drawn on a number of fronts today, as community after community enacts ordinances restricting in some way the ownership of a Pit Bull. Many of the major news magazines and the major television news programs have done stories on the breed with distorted information. As I see it, one of the problems about these stories is that the people who want to do the story already have in mind what they want it to be; so they edit everything accordingly so that it

does turn out as they had pre-conceived it. And I speak as one who has had experience with these groups.

Being human, I have my periods of doubt and depression, but luckily they are shortlived, for I try to keep in mind that things tend to run in cycles. I remember when California passed the first felony dog-fighting law. I was concerned about the law because it gave too much power to the humane groups, and I feared that innocent Bulldog owners would be harassed. Friends, worried that I would be one of the innocent victims caught up in it, urged me to move out of that "flaky state." Now, nearly every state in the union has a felony dog-fighting law much worse than the original California one. And, in the meantime, California has quietly rolled its law back to a misdemeanor.

Above: Rush Tango at 58½ pounds, undeniably in worthy form. *Opposite:* Cleo, three years old and 50 pounds, a bitch of Castelli and Johnson's Zebo breeding.

The Pretenders

The distinguishing characteristics of "Snarks" include: a meager and hollow taste, a habit of getting up late, and slowness in taking a jest. Not much more enlightening are distinguishing characteristics of breeds that are often confused with Pit Bulls. However, because confusion is so rampant, I thought I would take the time once again to try to clarify what breeds are similar to the APBT but are "light years" away from it. One absolutely distinguishing characteristic would be just which other breeds would an experienced pit-dog man utilize in a pit contest. The answer would be none! But even a pit-dog man might be fooled by the appearance of some of the breeds; however, he would soon ascertain by his game test that they were not suitable for his purposes, for that is the true essence of the American Pit Bull Terrier.

The Tibetan Mastiff can weigh up to 180 pounds; in its native land of China the breed is revered for its great power and willingness to defend its home and livestock. It has never been known as a rowdy rival to other dogs.

And a lifetime's experience with the breed has convinced me that all its other wonderful characerics either flow from that trait or are concomitant with it.

An important point to make here is that most breeds with which the public has any familiarity are show breeds. That is, they are breeds developed mainly for appearance. In most cases, the history of such a breed consists mainly of flights of fancy by one of its more influential devotees. It is these dogs, however, that are AKC-registered. To many people, the AKC-registered breeds are the purebred dogs and anything *not* registered by that body are suspect as a legitimate breed. Such is far from legitimate, as most of the best and most useful dog breeds are deliberately withheld from AKC registrations.

It should be noted that the AKC is finally coming under fire because of the deplorable breeding tactics that have been done under its auspices. Hip dysplasia, a cruel and crippling disease, is especially rampant in AKC stock, as is genetic blindness and a host of other inherited disorders. All these are a direct result of breeding strictly for looks and for sale without regard to other important traits.

It is not that I am disdainful of the AKC (well, maybe a *little*), for some of the breeds it registers (the Labrador Retriever, the Shetland Sheepdog, and the Dachshund, to mention just a few) are dogs I like. But look at even the breeds I name! (And truly, I did *not* think of this as I ticked the breed names off, as these really are dogs of which I am genuinely fond.) The Lab has dysplasia problems, the Shelties are wracked by blindness, and the Dachshunds frequently have back problems. But the main point I want to make is that the American Kennel Club is not the sole authority or registry of the dog world.

In any case, in discussing breeds related to the Pit Bull, I'll start with the breeds closest to it and work from there.

THE AMERICAN STAFFORDSHIRE TERRIER

In the case of the Am. Staf, we have a breed whose history really has a ring of authenticity to it. The breed started out as the AKC version of the American Pit Bull Terrier. In fact, it was John P. Colby's family (and Colby was one of the foremost breeders of American Pit Bull Terriers) that helped push for AKC recognition of the breed, for it was thought that the breed would become more popular under its auspices. The first dog registered was "Pete the Pup" of *The Little Rascals* fame. However, he was registered as a Staffordshire Terrier, as the AKC would not grant the other name for two reasons: One was that the AKC already had a Bull Terrier, and its adherents lobbied against including another "Bull Terrier"; two was that the AKC undoubtedly

The American Staffordshire Terrier is one of many bulldog breeds, not too distantly related to the American Pit Bull Terrier. Breeders today do not cross the two breeds, and hence they grow ever more distant as cousins. Photo by John Ashbey.

The Am. Staf (*left*) and the Staffordshire Bull Terrier (*right*) are two breeds of bulldog developed on opposite sides of the Atlantic. Once very similar in physical appearance, the two breeds now are noticeably different. Photo by Isabelle Français.

wanted to avoid granting the same name under which the United Kennel Club had registered the breed for years. (The UKC was the first big registry to recognize the APBT, and it was the first breed, in turn, to be recognized by the United Kennel Club. *All* the other breeds—including the Coonhounds—came later.)

But now, some fifty years later, the breed can no longer be considered the same. The reason? The breeds have been bred along entirely different lines. The result is the Am. Staf (the breed name was later changed to "American Staffordshire Terrier" to distinguish it from imported "Staffords"or Staffordshire Bull Terriers from England) is uniform in appearance, but its gameness ranges from none to very little. An occasional dog may turn up

that is truly game, but such an individual is so rare that he must be considered a freak of the breed. The gameness was lost because there was no way to know which individuals should be bred in order to preserve it. Staf owners were always foresworn never so much as to roll a dog, so there was no way to ascertain an individual's gameness.

Since appearance was to be the main manner in which the breed would be known, breeders had a tendency to breed for stocky, powerful-looking individuals that would stand up to people. After many years of experience, it is my opinion that an Am. Staf is more likely to bite a person than is an APBT. Crosses between the two breeds (which wouldn't even be considered crosses by many people) could very likely produce animals that could be dangerous to people, and they most assuredly would be known as "Pit Bulls"!

THE STAFFORDSHIRE BULL TERRIER

This is the English version of the old pit dog turned show dog. It was recognized a little over fifty years ago by The Kennel Club of Great Britain and was bred along show lines. It is smaller and stockier than the American Staffordshire.

In parts of the British Isles, badger baiting is legal; and this breed has been used for such participations. This was considered a game test by some fanciers—even though it would fall far short of a real game test, which uses another dog. Still, some English fanciers have told me that some dogs have been used for fighting over there and that many are game. However, it is generally agreed that they are not as game as the imported APBTs from America. Certainly, in my opinion, the Staffords imported and bred in Britain are not even as game as the Am. Stafs.

When the breed first began to be brought over during the early 1950s, it was generally believed that this was just another strain of the same breed. In fact, the AKC listed it as a Staffordshire Terrier; and some breedings were made, crossing the two breeds, and these were registered as Am. Stafs. One reason for these breedings was that many American Staf breeders thought the dogs were getting too big. A more predominant reason was likely the American fascination for imported dogs. However, one of the brightest, richest, and most influential of the American Staf breeders was Howard M. Hadley of Glendora, California,

An unusually colored Staffordshire Bull Terrier in Great Britain.

and he recognized that the breeds were not the same. He resisted the idea of the Stafford's being accepted as the same breed as its American counterpart, and, in the end, he prevailed. The Staffordshire Bull Terrier was recognized as a separate breed by the AKC.

Generally speaking, it has always seemed to me that the Stafford had an even better disposition with people than the Am. Staf, but he is even more of a caricature of the original pit dogs than the American show counterpart; that is, he is extremely squat, almost to the point of being grotesque. But, of course, that is the "cakes and ale" of show-dog people. They don't like dogs that look ordinary. The more grotesque, the better; and you can be sure that the show people will dream up some story of why the breed looks that way—just as they did with the Dachshund!

THE BULL TERRIER

Now here is the biggest pretender of them all, a breed that for years was the only one the public knew as a pit dog. In his show standard, it even says that this breed is the "gladiator" of the canine world. The truth is he is no such thing. Oh, of course, there was the concocted story of how the originator of the breed crossed one of the old Bull-and-Terrier types with some terrier and perhaps a Dalmatian to get cleaner lines and more agility—not to mention the white coloration. As the story goes, Hinks (the originator) matched one of his dogs against the old type, and not only did it win, but it did so with little harm to itself that it was able to win a dog show the next day. I'm sorry, but I don't believe a word of it!

The reason I am so skeptical is not entirely due to my innate perversity. The whole story simply smacks of the

An example of the Colored variety of the show Bull Terrier, a British breed created in the nineteenth century.

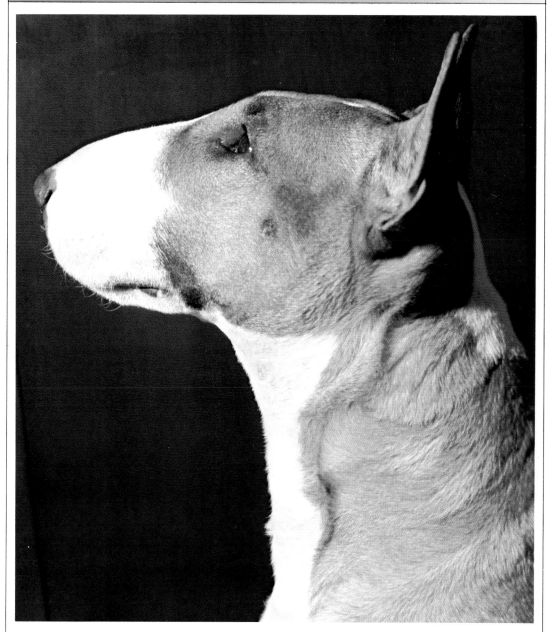

The Bull Terrier's muzzle is more elongated than that of many other bulldog breeds, which enabled the Bull Terrier to excel in a pit of rats. Photo by Isabelle Français.

type of thing that show dog people do. They have been known to make crosses for the sake of a certain appearance they wanted. But you don't do that with a competitive performance dog. For example, you wouldn't cross a racing Greyhound with a Pointer to obtain a better build. Crosses of any kind are doomed to produce slower Greyhounds, because that breed is simply the master of speed. You don't cross him for the same reason you don't cross a thoroughbred to a Morgan, an Arabian, or any other breed.

Now, here is what I think really happened, but, of course, it is just a guess; nevertheless, it is an educated guess in that it takes into account the tendencies of performance-dog people as opposed to show-dog people, and it is influenced by a lifetime of looking at artwork to puzzle things out. To begin with, there was a brachycephalic type of Bulldog that was kept and bred for the oddity of its appearance. Brachycephalic is the technical term for the pushed-in nose appearance of the modern show Bulldog and a number of other breeds, including the Boxer, Pug, King Charles Spaniel, Pekingese, and Bullmastiff, to mention just a few. In my opinion, this dog was crossed with some Terrier to produce the old "Bull-and-Terriers" or "Half-and-Halfs," as they were sometimes called. I think it was this "old type" that Hinks worked with to produce his "White Cavalier." It is even possible that they had a little match. Certainly, with those mouths, they wouldn't have been able to hurt each other! Anyway, I have seen drawings and paintings of Bull Terriers done in the late 19th Century which showed them with the brachycephalic nose. So it may indeed be true that the "Bull-and-Terrier" cross was made, but it influenced show dogs only, and was not an important landmark in the history of the modern APBT.

To give an example of how show-dog people rationalize show points (aspects of desired appearance), the Bull Terrier has a wide stance so that he is not easily taken off his feet; and he has those slanted eyes for protection from injury to them. But, in my opinion, what these people have ended up with is a wide-set, fat dog that can't see very well. And he can't fight his way out of a paper bag!

THE SHOW BULLDOG

Since all of these breeds have a certain relationship I end up covering the same ground, so the reader may bear with me if interested in this aspect of things—or skip over this part!

As I have stated many times, the American Pit Bull Terrier is the purest representative of the old-time Bulldog. He looks like him, and he does the same types of things that the old Bulldog was known to do. That is, he is the fighter without fear, he will run down and attack wild game—from boar to lion—and he will catch a bull or hog for a farmer and hold him until the farmer secures the animal.

Even in the modern APBTs, we have individuals showing up with aberrations of appearance. This is true, of course, with all breeds to a degree. However, there is a predictable pattern to some of the variations. For example, undershot dogs are by no means a rarity. The reason is that a dog that does the things which our dog does needs a strong lower jaw. Since there are natural variations on both sides of the ideal jaw, the strong mandible often results in an undershot dog. If

Opposite: **The show Bulldog of England first entered the conformation ring in 1860. Through selective crossing for desired characteristics, the Bulldog has had its appearance changed over the years. Note its large skull, rose-shaped ears, and undershot jaw.**

a dog is not undershot too badly, his bite (that is, the force of it) is not affected. However, if he is undershot to the extent that the lower teeth show, it is nearly always predictable that the dog will not have biting force.

Sometimes the condition is really extreme if the animal, in addition to being badly undershot, has a short muzzle. To me, it is easy to see how an especially extreme example of this could have occurred early on in the history of the old Bulldog; and the exotic and human-like appearance of such an animal might make him more likely to be kept as a pet and eventually turned into a show dog. In the world of show dogs, the exotic and grotesque are paramount.

It is a strange twist of irony that the "Bulldog" should end up with our breed's name officially in the AKC (and all other show-dog registries) and certainly in the public's mind. If what I think is true does indeed happen to be the case, it is possible that the "Bulldog" is just as pure a descendant of the old, historic Bulldog as is our breed. It is just that this one was bred away from the old type for the sake of appearance and fashion. Oh, to be sure, the characteristics were rationalized in typical show dog fashion. The brachycephalic trait is called "lay back," and it's supposed to help the dog breathe while it has hold of the bull. The wide stance is to give the dog leverage, when he has the bull by the nose. And perhaps

This English Bulldog and its pup illustrate the present-day show breed's more mellow temperament, compared to that of its pit-fighting ancestors.

This American Bulldog shows the strongly muscled, solid build that is characteristic of the breed. More of a working guard dog than a show dog, the American Bulldog maintains an active following in the U.S.

the tiny hindquarters are to give him agility at least at the back end! In any case, it is all nonsense. Anyone who has seen a catch dog work knows that the show Bulldog couldn't possibly do that kind of thing. The Bulldog simply has no mouth; he has very little to work with in grasping the bull. Besides that, he has no agility and no stamina. And I have yet to see one that has the inclination to do the work.

To many people, the modern show Bulldog has character all his own; and he is the national symbol of Britain. It gives me no pleasure to say anything against other breeds. But I would be remiss if I didn't at least give the facts. I mentioned before that the AKC happens to be receiving some criticism now for the

dogs that have been produced under its auspices. Unfortunately, the show Bulldog doesn't help its case any. Short-lived and dull-witted, the show Bulldog often must bear its young by Caesarean section because of the ridiculously small hindquarters having to give birth to the even more ridiculously large head.

THE AMERICAN BULLDOG

This breed is supposed to be a direct descendant of the old-time Bulldog. It may be true, but he certainly doesn't look like the paintings and woodcuts of the old Bulldog. Besides, there is little reason to believe that he is. A breeder in Georgia has been beating the drums for this breed, making the claim that it is in fact the old Bulldog. Pardon me for being

A Neapolitan Mastiff, half of Swinford's Bandogge creation. This is Ossa standing in front of owner's well-guarded and greatly prized Cherimoya tree.

skeptical, but I would like a little proof.

Still, although the breed is not yet recognized by the AKC, it may make the grade some day, as people seem to like the big rough-looking animals that these dogs are. They look something like a drop-eared Boxer, but are much larger, running between 80 to 100 pounds.

THE SWINFORD BANDOGGE

In this breed's case, there was no attempt to claim an ancient origin. The breed was started by a veterinarian named Swinford. It was a perfectly legitimate enterprise. People are always trying to improve upon what we have. Swinford was aware that the American Pit Bull Terrier was the supreme fighting dog, so he started out to make a better one. His theory, which certainly had its merits, was that if he could increase the size greatly, he would succeed. Not having the patience for trying to increase the size of the APBT by selective breeding, he bred a Neapolitan Mastiff bitch to a good American Pit

Bull Terrier male and then proceeded, with the help of friends, to try to develop a separate breed by selective breeding for size and gameness.

After ten years of this selective breeding, Pit Bull owners were challenged. One of them came up with a sixty-pound dog to go against one of the 130-pound behemoths, and the little dog chased the bigger one out of the pit at the twelve-minute mark.

THE AKITA

Now we come to some unrelated dogs; that is, they have no real relationship to the American Pit Bull Terrier other than the fact that they have allegedly been used for fighting. The Akita is obviously unrelated, as its appearance is that of the Spitz family of dogs (sled dog type), rather than the bulldog-mastiff appearance of so many of the other fighting dogs.

According to Carl Semencic, author of *The World of Fighting Dogs*, today's Akita breeders prefer to think of the Akita as a hunting dog. Semencic makes a convincing case for its being included in the fighting dog category, however, and I well recall, when the Akita first came to this country, its owners touted it as the breed that would dethrone the Pit Bull as the premier fighting dog of the country. It was, perhaps, after

A native Japanese breed, the Akita displays a plush coat, prick ears, and curled tail—suggestive of the breed's stemming from northern bloodlines. The Akita stands 24–28 inches high and weighs 75–110 pounds.

The Shar-Pei traces its roots to mainland China. In the 1970s, when very few specimens remained in existence, fanciers brought some of these dogs to the U.S., where the breed has prospered. When the Shar-Pei entered America, it was considered one of the rarest breeds in the world.

he failed to do this that his devotees decided that he was a hunting dog.

For some reason, the Japanese, who have sent us such excellent small cars, have a penchant for big dogs. The Akita is evidence of this, as the size of the breed often exceeds 100 pounds.

THE SHAR-PEI

This breed first came to the country as the Chinese Fighting Dog. It was supposed to be the end of the Pit Bull's fighting supremacy; and it, like the Akita, failed. In fact, it failed more miserably than all the others. Some now say that it was all a horrible mistake in the first place that anyone ever thought of this as a fighting breed. It was a mistake brought about by the mistranslation of some Chinese documents. Nevertheless, it is a breed that has been included in some of the bans on "fighting dogs" in certain "unenlightened" municipalities.

THE TOSA

Here is a *bona fide* fighting dog from Japan. Like the Akita, the Tosa is huge. In fact, it looks a little like a large and lippy APBT. I have only seen one of these dogs, and I was impressed with it. Most of the giant breeds are misbegotten animals, slow of wit, short-lived, and not so formidable as their owners think.

However, the Tosa is an exception to most of these, as he is a legitimate fighting dog that can be tough to whip. I am told by those who live in Asian countries, in which pit contests are legal, that the Tosa is not taken lightly by APBT owners. It is generally considered that it takes a Bulldog that is at least fifty-five pounds to whip one.

However, the sun may be setting on the Tosa as a fighting dog for the simple reason that even those enthusiasts in Japan are beginning to prefer the American Pit Bull Terrier. There is good reason for this. A smaller dog is a more convenient pet than a large one. And if he can whip the dogs that look so awesome, there is no need for him to look that way himself!

Once popular in the dog pits of Japan, the Tosa would fight to the death without ever uttering an audible syllable. The Tosa, selectively bred for size and silence, can weigh up to 200 pounds—truly an impressive dog.

Above: The shady, well-shaded Freeman's Rusty Red Boy. *Opposite:* Sam is owned by Gary McCurdy.

The Real McCoy

> *"A pound of pluck is worth a ton of luck."*
> JAMES A. GARFIELD

The *bona fide* American Pit Bull Terrier has more than luck and more than pluck. If he is, as I and many other APBT devotees believe, the most direct descendant of the old-time Bulldog, then he is the end product of countless centuries of breeding for pure courage. And that he has. In fact, he has something beyond courage—and that is called gameness.

"Gameness" is a term that is tossed around rather casually by sports commentators and writers and by people in general, but to the pit-dog man it has a very important meaning. It refers to that attribute of *never* giving up regardless of circumstances and conditions. The true, deep gameness that pit-dog men seek is not easily attained—but it is quite easily lost! Still, nearly all members of the breed have a measure of the trait that would astound the average person—even though it could be completely unimpressive to a pit-dog man.

The ideal of gameness takes a little getting used to, so perhaps it would be sufficient to say that it is the one trait that is most prized by pit-dog men. And it is my firm conviction, after over forty years of experience with the breed, that it is the Pit Bull's gameness that gives it its rock-steady disposition and its unique character which holds so many of us utterly entranced.

Of course, the American Pit Bull Terrier is best known as a fighting dog. And that he is. Naturally, he is other things, too, but there is no denying that he is the fighter *par excellence*. He is so good at his trade that it is difficult to convey just how good. Perhaps to say that he can whip any other breed of dog irrespective of size will suffice. However, even that somehow falls short of expressing the enormous and unique ability of this breed.

Now, I am perfectly aware that there are those who will say that fighting ability is of little consequence and that they are unimpressed by a dog that is good at it. Fine. I respect that opinion. Let them look elsewhere for a dog then. But let them also let us have our dog. They should have no quarrel with us as long as we keep our charges from pummeling theirs. It is true, of course, that the breed has other qualities, so that even those who would find his fighting abilities abhorrent might want him for his other traits. However, it is my firm conviction that no one should own one of these dogs who does not at least understand their desire to fight and ability to do so, and be willing to take the consequences for it: a little extra caution and care. If they are not so willing and accepting, then let them obtain another breed.

One way to illustrate just how good these dogs are is to tell the story of a man who is well known among pit fanciers in the United States. He was once a police officer in New York and later owned a plumbing business there. In his plumbing business, he came across all manner of dog owners, and, everyone knew that he owned Bulldogs. It so happened that there was a pit stationed in the basement of the plumbing business, so if someone came in with a dog that they thought could whip a Bulldog, he could be accommodated—those

were different times.

So all manner of dogs, from huge Rottweilers to Tosas to Airedales, were matched against Bulldogs. After years of doing this, the Bulldogs never lost a single match! Even I, who consider these dogs to be some sort of super canine, would not have predicted such an overwhelming outcome. What makes it all so impressive are these facts: First, the very best of the other breeds were brought in; the individuals didn't get there unless they were the absolute, outstanding, exceptional fighter for their breed. The Bulldogs, on the other hand, were usually the second-rate ones, as a pit-dog man is not going to waste a hot match prospect in a "pick-up" match against a cur dog. (Remember that "cur" is the term among the fancy for all breeds other than Bulldogs. No offense. It is simply a tradition that extends back into antiquity.) Another factor to take into account is that most pit dogs are kennel or chain dogs, and they don't get much exercise unless they're being conditioned for a match. Hence, all these dogs were Bulldogs that were being brought in for a fight against an invariably bigger adversary that had most likely had much better conditioning than the Bulldog. Finally, there is the matter of size. Most Bulldogs aren't all that big, and the best ones are usually small. Size difference isn't anything to be sneezed at, so it would seem that at least one other dog might be able to win simply on that basis. But it was never enough to overcome the incredible ability of the Bulldog.

One of the most amazing things to me is that none of the Bandogges ever won such a match. After all, the people who worked with those dogs were wealthy and educated people, and they were being guided by veterinarians who most assuredly

Dolly Danger pouncing through a field.

had some knowledge of genetics. You will recall that the breed was started off by crossing a good and well-bred Bulldog with a Neapolitan Mastiff, a breed that is supposed to be used for fighting in Italy. These huge dogs were selectively bred for ability and gameness for ten years before their owners challenged Bulldog owners. And even then, against these huge brutes, the Bulldogs, large and small, prevailed.

I was invited by a Chinese group to go to Taiwan. I was not able to make the trip because of a prior commitment. The head of the American Dog Breeders' Association went in my place. (He has since chided me good naturedly a number of times for passing up such an adventure to go to a mere science convention!) Anyway, one of the things Mr. Greenwood wanted to see was the Tosas. He saw very few. When asked where all the Tosas had gone, he was told that the Pit Bulls had killed them all. Well, maybe you aren't impressed by that, but I certainly am!

Besides defeating other canine breeds, the Bulldog proved himself, on both sides of the country, against timber wolves and wild dogs. On all the occasions involved, either a dog trainer or a veterinarian with an interest in canine ethology was the one providing the wild canids. It was never a contest in any of the instances, as the wolf or wild dog was simply a terrified animal, wanting nothing but to get away from the demon that had hold of him. It is instructive to remember that in the wild, animals don't really fight the way Bulldogs (or people) do. Their "fights" are mainly posturing or bluffing, technically known as a "threat display." If the situation actually deteriorates into a fight, it will be over quickly, and the victor aborts his attack upon receiving the "submission display" stimulus. It is a little more involved and technical than that, but you get the idea. The point is that we shouldn't be too surprised that these wild animals

Lundberg's Penny.

Bulldog guarding the premises!

were so terrorized by such a "professional" as the Bulldog. It should be pointed out that the timber wolf is a huge animal that will attack and bring down moose in the wild. I have seen films of them doing this, and it was truly impressive. The timber wolf also has much larger teeth than any breed of dog, and that fact has caused some consternation among scientists who believe the dog is descended from the wolf. There are a number of possible explanations for this, including that the origin of the dog was of a sub-species of wolf with smaller teeth; alternatively domestic dogs may have been selectively bred early to have smaller teeth and a curly tail to be distinguished from wild wolves. The sled dogs would be an example of this even today. The point is that the wolf is a truly formidable animal. The question is: could he whip a Bulldog if he would only stand and fight him? The answer is academic, for most assuredly one of the reasons the wolf runs is that he has not developed the ability to tolerate pain in the same manner as the Bulldog.

Another wild animal that the Bulldog has conquered is the wolverine, which has a reputation as a formidable animal. Two different people from Alaska and Canada have sent me pictures of Bulldogs doing battle with a wolverine—and whipping him!

If the wolverine doesn't impress you, how about a lion? After all, the lion, along with the Siberian tiger, is considered the most formidable animal of the order Carnivora. Even I would not expect the Bulldog to whip a lion one on one. Still, apparently it has happened on occasion. One such occasion was reported by Pierce Egan. A Bulldog and two crossbred Mastiffs were set upon a lion for sport back in Elizabethan England. The Mastiffs, according to Egan, were afraid to attack, and that left the little Bulldog to go in alone and seize the lion by the nose. This completely tamed the lion, and he simply tried to get away from the little Bulldog. There were other such events staged, and the Bulldog didn't always come out on top, but the fact that he did on even one occasion against such a

Bell's Dundee Jones is a son of Winn's Red Neck.

Ch. Crash, Son of Tombstone.

Left: Richard's General Stuart, better known as Jeb, is by Grand Champion Richard's General Fremont out of Champion Lar-San's Gypsy Rose. *Below:* Riptide Brendy is a six-year-old female.

Dacolias Tuco, a one-time pit winner and a son of Grand Champion Bad Billy.

Bellisle's Buddy and Bellisle's Chunk.

magnificent beast is a real cause for wonder. To be perfectly honest, I consider Pierce Egan's accounts to be generally unreliable, but so many things ring true in this story—such as the use of the nose hold and the idea that the lion would retreat from a dog—that they give the story some credibility.

Now, of course, we all know that the American Pit Bull Terrier is not made of steel; and he doesn't come from Krypton, so how does he pull off such amazing feats? Well, for one thing, if we accept the idea that he is descended from ancient times, we are not surprised that he is so good at his craft. We know Greyhounds to be an ancient breed that were depicted in ancient Egyptian friezes, so we are not astounded that this breed of dog is so much fleeter than any other. Because of his long history of selective breeding for speed, we would not try to challenge him with a more recent creation. But

in those same friezes are powerful-looking dogs on leads that were apparently used as kill dogs in the hunt. Since they look like large Bulldogs, it certainly does not seem unreasonable to suggest that perhaps our dogs are direct descendants of those ancient canines. Thus, the Bulldog has traits that took more than a few generations to develop.

One of the traits is the all-important gameness, a complex trait that involves a tolerance to pain, which is probably brought about by an unusual ability to immediately generate endorphins in the brain of the animal. It also involves a sturdiness and ability to absorb punishment without serious consequences. All game dogs seem to have an ability to pace themselves just right, to be able to gauge their opponents accurately and pace themselves accordingly. They also know when the opponent is sagging

Kitty with her stick.

A Pit Bull outjumps two English Bull Terriers.

and, thus, when to pour on the heat.

Bulldogs are cool under pressure, certainly under fighting conditions at least, and they are thus able to learn new techniques, which they practice in future rolls or fights. This ability to learn is so pronounced that it is often the first thing that is commented upon by a newcomer who has never seen a roll or a pit contest before. Invariably, they say something along the lines of, "I didn't expect them to be so smart!" Other advantages besides the natural inclination to learn would include the agility, speed, strength, and grace that would be expected to give an individual dog the edge in a fight. A natural feel for balance and leverage also seems to be a part of the make-up of the breed.

The American Pit Bull Terrier, though, is more than a mere fighting machine—good as he is at it. The same traits that make him the incomparable fighter he is make him an excellent pet. Although owners must take extra precautions with him, the Bulldog is a good pet: he is shorthaired and clean; and contrary to the public belief, he has an absolutely reliable disposition, and is eager to please. You don't have to worry about his guarding his food so fiercely that you are afraid to take his food bowl away from him. If he is injured in some way, you don't have to worry about his biting you out of pain and fear, as many dogs of other breeds will. Almost all Bulldogs are very quiet dogs which seldom bark. Strangely enough, while they are tireless companions in any form of play, most of them are not hyperactive, so they are relatively sedate house dogs.

If you want him to be more than a house dog, there are certainly other uses for him. And I am not speaking here about illegal pit fights. He can be used legally in many areas for hunting. Check your state hunting laws, but most states allow you to use a dog in hunting wild boar or raccoons. A Bulldog won't give you the beautiful "voice" of a hound on the trail of a raccoon, for he is a silent trailer (that is, he doesn't make a sound while trailing). Such dogs are usually more successful than open trailers at actually trapping the raccoon. Personally, however, I like raccoons and all wild animals, and I am not inclined to hunt them.

Naturally, a Bulldog can't be expected to have the excellent "cold nose" of a well-bred scent hound; however, I should point out that not too long ago a Pit Bull won the national field trial contest for treeing hounds. In such contests a cold nose and beautiful baying voice are not part of the competition, but speed on the trail, hustle and intensity are; and that is the reason why a Bulldog could win a Coonhound trial. A Bulldog has such hustle and intensity that he is likely to climb up that tree after the coon!

Most people are going to want the dogs mainly as pets. For the person who is willing to take a responsible attitude about the dog, he can be the most satisfying and fulfilling of all dog breeds in this capacity. Howard Hadley once told me, many years ago, that there was something about these dogs that tended to get in a person's blood. Once having owned a Bulldog, people in general simply are not able to settle for anything else. After years of personal experience with countless dogs and countless people, I have discovered that he was truly correct. These dogs really are spoilers. A Collie may be more beautiful and a Manchester more convenient, but they aren't as much fun.

Although friendly with humans, this dog reacts to the presence of a strange dog. Considering a dog vicious because he is aggressive towards other dogs is of the same mentality as condemning rat terriers because they go after rats.

Lance's Little Gobbler on top of Cadillac Mountain in Maine. Owner, Lance J. Levy.

Above: **J.R. "Dick" Colby with Primo, a very important dog, as he was the basis for the Staffordshire Terrier breed standard.** *Opposite:* **The famous Winn's Red Neck, also known as Idle Times T.J.**

The Fancy

"Toward no crimes have men shown themselves so coldbloodedly cruel as in punishing differences of belief."
JAMES RUSSELL LOWELL

"There is so much good in the worst of us,
And so much bad in the best of us,
That it ill behooves any of us
To find fault with the rest of us"
ANONYMOUS

The "fancy" is a term that strikes my fancy, but it hasn't been used for many years as a regular term, which shows, I suppose, that even in the pit-dog game terms do change—even though some stick with us from antiquity. Anyway, the word "fancy" was used from Victorian times, and possibly much earlier, to a mere three decades ago to refer to those people involved with the American Pit Bull Terrier. Of course, that meant primarily people who were involved with the pit-dog game, but even those who just kept the dogs as pets were accepted in earlier days. Such is not the case today because of different circumstances. For one thing, there are a lot more owners of Bulldogs as pets, and not all of them approve of pit contests. (They didn't in earlier days either, but they were more tolerant.) And, for two, pit-dog men must be much more secretive in these days than they were just a few decades past.

My purpose in this chapter is to give an overview of serious owners of the dogs. This will include not only pit-dog men and boar hunters, but an attempt will be made to include many serious and responsible owners.

I first came upon the Bulldog scene in 1944 when I was thirteen

in its pages, and it seemed to me that the breeds encompassed by the UKC were dogs primarily used for something other than show, as American Pit Bull Terrier, English Shepherds, and six varieties of Coonhounds were featured. That was about the same time that I was beginning to realize that there was much more fanciful thinking than fact to the histories and capabilities

From left to right: Tom Byron, John P. Colby, Patsy Reardon (head of Boston Water Department at that time), and Henry Cooligan in a picture of APBT fanciers taken about 1920.

years old. I had already had experience with a number of breeds but had been primarily interested in Collies (the show type—as was the case with so many people, I was completely unaware of the *real* Collie, the Border Collie). When I became a subscriber to *Bloodlines Journal,* the official publication of the United Kennel Club, all the registry's breeds were represented

of the show-dog breeds.

In any case, a lot has changed since then and yet traditions are strong with the APBT breed. For that reason, many of the old ones, along with terminology that obviously has ancient roots, manage to stay on even to these days. I will touch upon a few of them and on those that have changed in the mere forty-five years that I have observed the game.

Garner's Tom, a Colby dog.

To set the scene, let me give a few facts that are known. Back in Ireland and England, and probably the other lands from which the Bulldog came, it was rare for a person to have a kennel full of dogs. The people just didn't have the land or resources for doing that. So they often worked within a family of real relatives, each one keeping one or two dogs, and cooperating in breeding programs. Sometimes the "family" consisted of a group of unrelated individuals. Whatever the case, the people were bound together by their dedication to the dogs, and the term "family dogs" was often used to refer to imports. The term "old family" originally referred to any of a number of bloodlines that belonged to a particular individual's family of fighting dogs.

One of the most respected of the old-time dog men in the U.S. was Jim Corcoran, who had come for the purpose of meeting John L. Sullivan in a heavyweight championship fight. Sullivan lost the title when he tried to defend it under the new rules, and Corcoran was strictly a bare-knuckles fighter, so he stayed in the country and eventually became a Boston police captain. He sent back for dogs from his "old family" and a good many of our dogs—possibly all—trace back to those imports. Of course, the breed was already here, but Corcoran's dogs were generally superior to the individuals in his area.

The attitude of the time was to "guard the blood," as each group thought that his bloodline was the superior one. The pit-dog game was dominated by people of Irish and English descent, although there were plenty of people of all nationalities involved. In the early days, nearly everyone who owned a Bulldog had some connection with the pit, for it was not easy to obtain one as a mere pet. Most of the people who owned the dogs but were not actually engaged in contesting them had, as housepets, dogs that were "hide-away" dogs for pit-dog men, and were considered an "ace in the hole" for men who might lose a key dog in their bloodline (or their "family's" bloodline). The breed itself was considered secret and special. Anyone who would sell dogs to the general public was immediately branded a peddler, or worse, and was pretty much ostracized from the dog game (which,

incidentally, was referred to simply as "the game").

John P. Colby of New England was the first successful dog person to break that unwritten rule: Thou shalt not sell a dog to a non-pit-dog person. He openly advertised the dogs in a variety of publications and did his best to popularize them.

Perhaps one of the reasons Colby was able to break with tradition was that he himself was no immigrant, and his parents were not dog people. His father and other relatives had worked on the old clipper ships back in the days when the only power was the wind. As a young lad of twelve, John P. Colby witnessed his first pit-dog contest. The friend he went with had the losing dog. Colby became an active participant in finding a dog to defeat the winner. Before long, he

Mike Colby with a pure white Colby dog.

The great Colby's Galtie is shown in a very rare and extremely old photo.

Colby's Galtie

really had the fever. He began to sell dogs at a young age, at a time when the pit-dog men were perhaps more forgiving of such things since he was just a boy. Still, he had a knack for selective breeding, and he had the connections to obtain good foundation stock. In the town of Newburyport, Massachusetts, the Irish were pouring in because of the potato famine crisis in Ireland. Many of them brought their Bulldogs with them, as there was little extra cost to bringing a dog along.

It's my speculation that Colby was able to pull off the idea of selling dogs to the general public because he was selling quality dogs, animals that pit-dog men themselves would be happy to have. And, of course, pit-dog men bought them, too. Although there were some references to Colby as a peddler, he pretty much escaped being tarred by that brush.

Colby's Merle
1948

Colby's Merle, also known as Vose's Merle, as the Colbys let Vose utilize her for a while as a brood bitch before getting her back.

One of the reasons had to be that the strain itself became so desired because of its quality and has since become the best known of all strains. Even Staf people don't bad-mouth Colby, but I wonder how many of them know that Colby's Primo was the model for the Staf standard. And I wonder how many Stafs measure up to Primo in conformation—and, of course, we won't even compare gameness!

Other members of the fancy, to be sure, occasionally advertised and sold dogs. But they didn't escape the peddler image. Earl Tudor of Oklahoma couldn't have cared less about his image, and he sold dogs all his life. Not too much was said about him, as he was in his own little group in the redlands of Oklahoma; and he was small but as tough as they come. He also had a certain charisma that drew would-be prospects to him; and

they listened to him as though he were a god. He claimed never to be a breeder, but many great dogs passed through his hands, and he made breedings with them. Howard Heinzl was a connection between Colby and Tudor, though the men were of basically different eras. Heinzl hailed from Chicago and credited John P. Colby with getting him righted from a bad start. Heinzl considered Colby scrupulously honest in every way—including the keeping of his breeding records. However, Heinzl was also a great admirer of Earl Tudor, although he acknowledged that Tudor made little effort to keep accurate records—in fact, he at times deliberately wrote misleading pedigrees.

Men like McClintock, Saddler, Wallace, Lightner, and Hemphill were breeders of the old school, breeding dogs only for themselves and their friends and family. And to this day, there persists the name "peddler," which is very likely to be applied to anyone who sells his pit-dog stock to the general public. However, there exist almost no dogs of the bloodlines of the people just named, while most of the present-day dogs trace back to Colby, Tudor, and Corvino breeding, all of whom sold dogs regularly and for a lengthy period.

Even to this day Bulldog people who sell their stock regularly are automatically dismissed as "peddlers," and it can be a tough rap to take even in these days. Thus, in an important way, the Bulldog fanciers differ from devotees of other breeds, who find no shame whatsoever in making breedings and selling the pups to anyone with the money. Such a situation also makes it very difficult for neophytes—and reporters—to find out the straight

Above: "Robert Newton, as Bill Sykes, gazes ruefully at film's canine star, 'Relyon Jake the Rake.' Dog plays role of a toughie." *Below:* Colby's Spook.

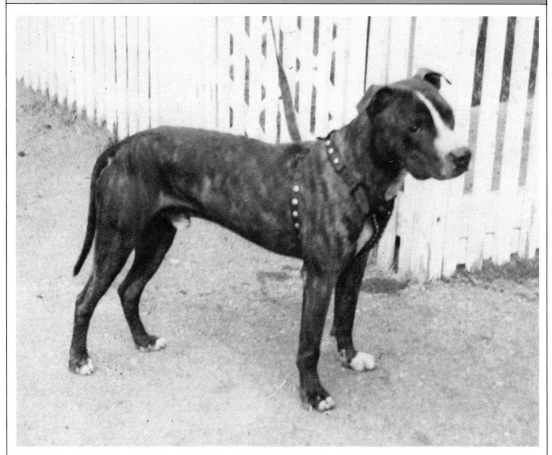

Colby's Primo, Jr., one of the great Colby stud dogs and the sire of the author's first Bulldog.

scoop on the dogs.

It has been popular to portray the pit-dog people in the newspapers and on television shows as sadistic and ill-educated people. There must be somebody out there somewhere who conforms to that stereotype. However, I have never met even one who fits it. Certainly, there have been many I thought didn't measure up to what an owner of these dogs should be; however, I have known none who really felt nothing for the dogs or who wanted to see them suffer. On the other hand, I have known countless dedicated dog men who centered their entire lives around the dogs. They were either dedicated breeders or pit-dog men,

that is, men who were interested only in fighting the dogs.

There is a difference between the men who are most interested in matching dogs and those who are most interested in the breed and in improving or preserving it through breeding. The point is well made in a story told by Bobby Hall in his book, in which he mentions someone talking about breeding when Maurice Carver interrupted to say, "Bobby doesn't know a thing you're talking about. He's a dog-fighter, not a breeder." Of course, some men manage to straddle both categories, but they are rare. Most dog men tend to be either one or the other. Apparently, each activity demands

Frank A. Ferris's Mac, a straight Colby dog. Ferris was once owner of the American Dog Breeders' Association, having purchased it from Guy McCord, the founder, and Greenwood later purchased it from Ferris.

Mangrum's Shorty with the trophies that she won as a pit dog. She was a descendant of the great White Rock dog.

personality traits that exclude the other. But both these groups are dependent upon each other in a sort of symbiotic relationship. Breeders need pit-dog men to test their stock for them; and pit-dog men certainly need breeders to provide them with animals they will utilize in their activities. The two groups have different characteristics, and I'll try to delineate some of them to show how they do differ in attitudes.

Breeders are the ones to whom the only excuse for dog-fighting is as a means of perpetuating a breed of dog that they consider one of the greatest animals that has ever walked the earth. They take great pride in the breed, and they are downright fanatical in developing a quality strain. Many of the greatest breeders never fought a dog in their lives. A few of them, such as Bob Wallace, John P. Colby, Bob Menefee, and Dan McClintock,

occasionally matched a dog to test the quality of the strain. However, many simply left it up to the men who were actively engaged in constantly matching dogs to do the testing for them. It is characteristic of such breeders that they grudgingly give a dog up for fighting purposes and make themselves a pain in the neck constantly checking up on the animal and offering a lot of not necessarily desired advice in the matching and conditioning of a prospect. Breeders complain about the quality of the people in the pit-dog game. They believe the best breed deserves the best people, and, of course, they obtain a somewhat jaundiced view of pit-dog men, because they are bound to have a few bad experiences with the number of dogs they let out.

Pedigrees become second nature with breeders; breeders are the ones who always ask what the breeding is

Sandy Keller demonstrates that Bulldogs don't need a kitten to get them to run a treadmill. A stuffed unicorn works fine! (And most dogs will run on the mill for the sheer fun of it.)

on a dog—and they remember! If a dog has done particularly well in the pit, and no one knows how it is bred (a not altogether unknown occurrence), it is the breeder who will go to great lengths to try to find the answer to the mystery. And it is he who is so frustrated if the breeding can not be known.

It has been my observation that it is the breeder who sticks with the dog hobby, while the pit-dog man is

come to mind as pit-dog men who went the distance with the dogs, never giving up on them, but sometimes becoming impatient when there were lean times as far as getting a dog matched was concerned. Although not caring as much about pedigrees as the breeder, the pit-dog man is usually aware of what type of breeding he likes; but many dislike trying to stick with a given strain. "Game dogs are

Charles Dunn uses his Bulldog Rick as a combustion engine.

more likely to tire of things and find another hobby. Now, this is only my opinion, and indeed it would be difficult to prove, because the situation becomes muddled, for many pit-dog men (dog-fighters) eventually become breeders. They make the complete metamorphosis, too, disdaining the matching of dogs and becoming hypercritical of those who do, in the sense that they are quick to criticize any perceived misjudgments and anything other than royal treatment for the dogs.

On the other hand, the pit-dog men are the "action men," as they call themselves. They aren't always flashes in the pan either, as several of them have spent a lifetime at the sport. Earl Tudor and Bert Clouse

where you find them" was an old saying of Tudor's; and it is a philosophy embraced by most pit-dog men. They really don't care how a dog was bred so long as he was game and can be relied upon to win. Unlike the breeder, the "action man" is less demanding about gameness. If a dog can win, that is, if he has enough ability coupled with enough gameness to beat his opponents, that is all the pit-dog man asks for. A breeder is more of a purist than that, as he will tend to be less impressed by a multi-match winning pit-dog if his gameness is unproven and if his pedigree is unimpressive.

One thing about the pit-dog man is that he finds the "game" absolutely

Jeff Burke with Hilliard/Mim's Ruby Red.

Right: Barny and Horus work at being photogenic. *Below:* Sorrell's Hurt, a two-time winning pit dog who also became a show dog and weight-pulling ace.

fascinating. I have actually met many who really believed that there was a conspiracy to keep dog-fighting from the public because it would be too attractive to them. Our pit-dog man can't believe any other way than that everybody else would be as enthralled by the activity as he is. Consequently, letting the public in on it would be a serious blow to other spectator sports! (Now, of course, this is not a belief of all pit-dog men, not even of a majority of them; however, it is certainly more prevalent among the dog-fighters than among the breeders.) Because of his fascination for the game, the pit-dog man doesn't mind all the work entailed in conditioning a dog for a match. He enjoys the companionship and joint venture that is involved in taking a dog through his keep (training period), running with him, working him, and doing agility drills with him.

Pit-dog men vary in the methods they utilize for conditioning. Some disdain the treadmill, training machine, and swim tanks, and rely on simple roadwork. Others utilize all methods in order to obtain a well-rounded and completely conditioned animal. These men (and sometimes women) feel they develop a special relationship with a dog in the keep, one that is unequaled in closeness in any other human-dog partnership. For the pit-dog, it is a situation new to him, one in which he receives nearly eight hours a day of constant attention. He enjoys it and enjoys the work. And he does seem to become quite close to his handler, who is taking him through his keep and will eventually be in the pit with him when he meets his opponent.

There are ways that the two groups are quite similar, and, as I have mentioned before, there is a certain overlapping of traits. Also mentioned before was the fact that a few men have been able to straddle the line, being a member of both groups. George Saddler, George Armitage, and Maurice Carver immediately come to mind as examples of such people.

Whichever group dog men belong to, there are certain general characteristics that apply to most of them. First, they are honest-to-goodness dog lovers. To many people, such a thing might seem impossible, but it is true nonetheless. Other dog devotees, such as sled-dog people, hunting-dog fanciers, and herding-dog aficionados would tend to understand that statement more than the average pet owner of dogs and certainly more than show-dog people. However, it must be admitted that in all dog competitions, from pit-dogs to show dogs, a natural objectivity eventually develops, and what could only be described as a more detached attitude has to be developed in such endeavors. I don't find this "detached attitude" or "hardness," if you prefer, more prevalent among Bulldog people than among those of other competitive dog activities, including showing dogs.

Being a closed society formed around a clandestine activity, the pit-dog game has some ancient terminology and traditions that still apply today. I have already touched upon the stance of looking down upon those who sell dogs, but there are other things too. For example, a Bulldog man nearly always addresses a fellow dog man as friend in the salutory part of a letter (e.g., "Friend Stratton"). This practice, I'm convinced, originated in the fact that the dog game encompasses people of all walks of life—from criminals to respected professional people. The term "friend" denoted that the other person was a true comrade in the

Some Pit Bulls don't mind being chained up.

dog fraternity (often called simply the "fraternity"), irrespective of differences in social and educational status.

A pit-dog person in the past would usually sign off a letter as "Your friend," but today there has been a shift to "Yours in sport," though the people who have been in the dog game longer still disdain that phrase. What is amusing is that even people who have nothing whatsoever to do with the pit-dog game, such as show-dog people and weight-pull fanciers, will also use that term. It's new and not generally used by the real pit-dog people.

The custom of calling the American Pit Bull Terrier "Bulldog" extends back as far as I've been able to trace, that is, well over a hundred years. Pit-dog people have always been able to switch over to "Bull Terrier," "Pit Terrier," and even "Pit

Cathy and Randy Street and Heinzl's Trudy. Owner, Martin Street.

Lance's Little Gobbler. Owner, Lance J. Levy.

Bull" when writing formally or speaking to someone outside the fancy (or the "fraternity"). John P. Colby's original stationery had a heading that said "Fighting Dogs" and under that "Bull Terriers." George Armitage in his book, *Thirty-five Years with Fighting Dogs*, refers to the dogs as "Bull Terriers," and when he wants to discuss the show Bull Terrier that we all know as such, he calls it the "English Bull Terrier." The name "American Pit Bull Terrier" became in vogue more as the formal name for the breed as the United Kennel Club grew and made its influence felt. The American Dog Breeders' Association registered the dogs as "Pit Bull Terriers," but they later changed the designation to "American Pit Bull Terrier." The only difference then was that the UKC placed the "Pit" part of the name in parentheses, and the ADBA left out the parentheses. Later, the UKC eliminated the parentheses, too.

A term that has changed since I've been associated with the dogs was that of referring to a dog's canine teeth as "tusks." Now they are more often called "cutters"; but that term is certainly unsatisfactory, as dogs don't slash and cut. After a fight or a roll, they may end up with cuts, but those are caused by a dog seizing and shaking. A dog mostly has holes after a fight. A more satisfactory term for the canines is simply that, "canines," in view of the fact that "tusk" is no longer used (except by the very, very old timers!). I'll admit that tusk certainly sounds a little odd, and I have no idea when that term came into use.

A time-honored custom in the game is that the source of the dog always has the right of first refusal. For example, if someone sells you a dog, and there comes a time that you must divest yourself of the animal, you must offer him back to the person you bought him from for the same price you paid. If the dog was given to you, then you offer it back free. Failure to comply with this simple code is seen as very poor manners.

Pollard's Satan "Mike."

Now, of course, the fancy refers to those people who are involved in some way with the pit activity of the breed. There are other people involved with the breed, including hunters and farmers, who utilize the dogs as stock dogs or catch dogs, and, more recently, there have been added to this non-pit category the weight-pull enthusiasts and show-dog people. In fact, their publications outnumber the publications dedicated to the pit-dog game. The attitude of the non-pit people varies from tolerance of the game to outright disapproval. (Though I rarely come across anyone in any category of the Bulldog fraternity *who understands and has attended pit contests* who is hostile to the idea of matching the dogs, although they themselves, for various reasons, may want no part of it.)

An important question might be: What is the attitude of the participants—that is, the members of the fancy—about their own participation in something as reviled as the matching of fighting dogs? The truth is that it varies somewhat. Some individuals feel helplessly caught in the clutches of a compulsion over which they have no control. They even remark, only half jokingly, that "We all have a defect in our personalities." Others feel absolutely self-righteous about their sport; and, if the public has problems with it and doesn't understand it, that is *their* problem. As far as they are concerned they are involved in an ancient and noble pastime that has produced the greatest of canines.

It has been my observation that most pit-dog people are quite religious and inclined toward conservatism in politics. I suppose the religious part stems from the fact that so many of the old-time pit-dog

Working over a steel-belted tire is just plain play for the dog.

men were immigrant Irish and thus Catholics. Another part has it roots in the fact that pit fighting has been especially popular in what H. L. Mencken called the "bible belt" part of the country. In any case, it is my opinion that many of the dog men are quite religious. In fact, there were two that I knew who were ministers. One became a born-again Christian, and the particular religion to which he belonged put the onus on its followers to obey the law of the land—irrespective of how a person felt about them. This individual dutifully gave up matching dogs. But he did hold onto his dogs, as he still admired them, and he hadn't changed his mind about there being nothing wrong with matching dogs. He was simply obeying his religion.

I personally am not very religious, being of the "scientific persuasion," so I am not trying to place a halo over the fanciers by declaring them as generally of a religious bent. It is simply one more step in trying to present the absolute truth about the American Pit Bull Terrier and his followers.

Above: Ironman's Snookie, a descendant of Boomerang on both sides of his pedigree. *Opposite:* Zeus, owned by Nick Pisano, is by Giroux's Champion Rocky out of Saleem's Boom Boom.

The Game

> *"Do what you love. Know your own bone; gnaw at it, bury it, unearth it, and gnaw it still."*
>
> THOREAU

There have undoubtedly been many pit-dog men who have decided the dog game was too rough. It was not for them. It was not their "bone." After all, not only is a pit-dog man an automatic pariah in society, he is subject to persecution and prosecution by a society that is in the throes of hysteria about something of which it knows nothing. But the American Pit Bull Terrier breed, that is something else. It is truly what he lives for. Anyone who knows anything at all about the breed knows that to be true. For that reason, I have argued that the contesting of dogs is not cruel. I haven't bothered to argue the morality of it, because many people are still caught up in the idea that it is a cruel and monstrous game practiced by the scum of the earth. Well, they may not all be the salt of the earth—though some of them are!—but, most assuredly they are not all scum. They are dog people not unlike other dog people. And I think it ill behooves those of us who find the American Pit Bull Terrier to be the finest of dogs to condemn the people who help preserve him as he is. Should the game be condemned then? Well, let's take a look at what has been said about it, compare it with other dog activities, and show it as it really is.

First of all, the people who have been describing the pit-dog game for the general public don't know what they're talking about; and they seem to have little integrity about representing their knowledge as fact. For example, Maxwell Riddle, a columnist for *Dog World Magazine* and an author of many fine books on dogs, has made several comments on the pit-dog game. One column stated that pit-dogs were made to stare at each other until they became enraged. That simply is not so. It was an honest mistake, as I think perhaps Mr. Riddle had been to a cockfight or two, and he believed that pit-dog contests must be started off in a similar way—but they aren't. He shouldn't represent such a thing as personal knowledge.

But Mr. Riddle (whose writings, incidentally, I do enjoy) is a very mild transgressor compared to "the regulars." Not too long ago *Dog Fancy Magazine* ran a feature by one of their regular columnists describing a typical dog-fight. What was funny was that the column was entitled "Dog-fighting—Take a Stand." Then a scene was described that no one could favor, and readers were invited to write in to vote whether they were for or against it! Some of the fallacies presented were: that a regular pit was rarely used; that the fights actually took place out in the backwoods; and that when the handlers led their dogs to the place of the fight, they kicked them repeatedly (the reason stated was that "mean dogs win"). Since just a few issues previously that

Yankee Boys' Bean is by Poncho out of Shosty, a daughter
of the great Jeep dog.

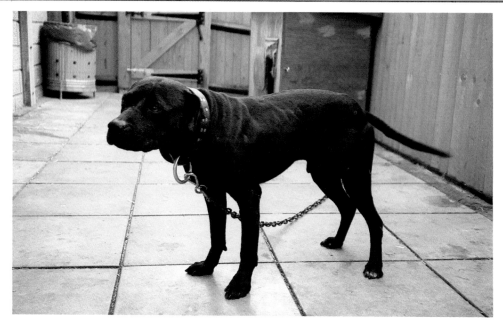

Dirty Harry's Hector.

Slater's Bad Baby.

magazine had solicited an article on the "Bull Terrier breeds" from me (one that I was only too happy to write), I wrote the editor and told him some day I would point out the fallacies in the dog-fighting article. I never did do that, because when I looked at the article closely, it had no truths in it whatsoever, which meant that the author was an

of this cows the dog—something a pit-dog man would certainly not want before a fight. Besides that, mean dogs don't usually win. They lose because they quit. A sound disposition seems to go with gameness. Therefore, nice dogs win for the simple reason that almost all Bulldogs—and especially the game ones—are nice dogs. They're "good

Broadway Shanty, a one-time winner sired by Champion Drummer.

absolute charlatan. All the more reason, I suppose, to write to the editor and expose him; however, I had a feeling it would be a waste of time, and I wouldn't enjoy doing it.

When an old friend of mine who does match dogs and has done so for years called me long distance, I read the article to him over the phone. He chuckled through most of it, at times breaking out into a hearty laugh; but when I got to the part about the handlers kicking their dogs, he said the very thing I had been saying, "Not only does that guy not know Bulldogs, he doesn't even understand the nature of dogs." What he meant by that was that dogs aren't made mean by kicking them. That's a popular fallacy. The effect

guys"!

Other representations have been even more bizarre. About fifteen years ago, when the hysteria about the pit-dog game first began, it was fomented by people who wrote that pit-dog men trained their charges by "baiting" them with kittens and puppies. In the fights themselves, they forced the dogs to fight by the use of cattle prods. To "blood" the dogs, pigeon blood was poured on them to bring out their blood instinct, I suppose, to get them ready for the fight. The fighting dogs themselves were likely to be of any breed; in fact, most of them were mixed breeds with a streak of viciousness in them. Other accounts related that the "Pit Bull" was the

Carter's Champion Sunday.

main event dog, while other breeds from Labrador Retrievers to Doberman Pinschers were the "preliminary event." In one "eyewitness" account, it was described how one Labrador Retriever slashed open the belly of another, and the handler simply dropped the dog by the side of the pit, not even having the decency to put a bullet through its head to end its suffering. Other accounts tell of losing handlers taking their dogs out and shooting them after the contest, because they were so enraged at being associated with a losing animal.

Now, of course, all these accounts can't be true, for some cancel each other out. Nonetheless, the accounts are meant to be overwhelming—and they are, to me at least. It is not the shock of the accounts themselves that overwhelm, however, but the cool insolence of the writers who propagate such nonsense and expect the public to believe it. And the sad truth is that the public has generally bought the whole circus. One of my own nieces told me how a police officer informed her that her lost puppy had probably been stolen by dog-fighters for training fighting dogs, as they had been having a lot of trouble with that!

The public can't really be blamed for believing all these things, as most people just don't know about the true nature of dogs themselves, let alone that of the American Pit Bull Terrier. Besides, they are bombarded from all sides with these stories and variations of them. Television dramatizations and news documentaries have given credence to them.

Nevertheless, it would seem to me that a thoughtful and analytical person would look at these stories and eventually come to the conclusion that they are a scam, for they can't *all* be true. They really do

cancel each other out. One account says a pit is not used. Another describes the pit and tells how a blood-stained carpet, laden with urine and fecal matter, is used. Another point is that it would seem obvious that only that which would discredit the pit fights is used. For example, many accounts picture the pit scene as being one of prostitution and drug peddling. It is emphasized that big money is bet on the fights; hence, the fights don't merely constitute cruelty to animals but are part of a big, illegal gambling ring.

Before I describe a true picture of the game, let me make just a couple of points. First, in my opinion, the purveyors of this nonsense have not only lied, but they have done so knowingly, with cool calculation, and with obvious contempt for the truth and the public. Let's face it, these people are staking their reputations on that which they are saying is the truth. They are claiming to be

Any Bulldog will be fine with a cat if it is raised with it.

eyewitnesses to some of the nonsense just described. Now, I can empathize and socialize with an animal rights advocate, for I am one myself. But I have no time for out-and-out charlatans—especially when they are doing it for their own self-aggrandizement and to line their own pockets. Look at the harm they do! Isn't it bad enough to have a puppy or little dog being lost without having images of it being torn apart

caught someone training a pit dog with cats or little dogs. Can they help realizing that they themselves were the inspiration of such atrocities?

When I tell of the pit-dog game, I am painting a picture as it really is among *bona fide* dog men. One of the problems of the humaniacs is that they want to put everyone in one bag, from the street gangs who have discovered the Bulldog (thanks to our humaniacs' tales in the news

Kitty and Honey with neighborhood fan club.

by a fighting dog running through your mind over and over? And consider that, admittedly, the images portrayed by the media of the American Pit Bull Terrier are going to appeal to sick minds and disreputable people generally. Every time a sensationalistic piece appears in the media, it inspires countless miscreants to obtain a Bulldog. And the charlatans who fed the media the information have told them how to train it: Simply obtain kittens, puppies, and little dogs. Eventually our humaniacs will be able to say with truth that they have

media) to the "dope heads" who turn their dogs loose on any canine unlucky enough to pass the way of their Bulldogs. Bulldog owners need not and should not all be tarred with the same brush because of the misdeeds of a few. Are thoroughbred owners thrown in with all those who own horses and possibly mistreat them?

At this point, let me leave the ravings of the unscrupulous lunatics and make an attempt to return to the world of reality. Here is a true picture of the game as best I can tell you.

Nick's Commanche.

When a pit-dog man decides that he has a prospect worthy of matching, he has done so on the basis of having rolled his dog a number of times and observed that he is a better fighting dog than the average. He has not had to utilize kittens and puppies in his training. Indeed there would be no point in that, and the young pit dog probably would not even do anything to the puppy; he most likely would have played with it. As for kittens, Bulldogs are no more cat chasers than ordinary dogs; however, if they do have such an inclination, they are much more deadly at it. So, a certain number of cats could be utilized to let a Bulldog kill, but what would be the point of it? This *would be* inexcusably inhumane and the dog is learning nothing that is going to help him as a pit dog. I personally have always liked cats, and I would never defend the dog game if cats were really utilized in training.

One of the reasons for opening the dog up to match is to ascertain how he measures up with the best of what the other guys are breeding from their strains. If not for the guy who is matching the dog, it is being done for

Dharma ridding yard of garden snake.

Stevens' Murphy, a brother to Champion Bessie, won one match and was voted best in show.

the breeder who bred him. Our pit-dog man estimates what will be the most efficient fighting weight for his dog and he opens him up at that weight. Of course, he can't do it through any publication. He simply lets friends in the dog game know he has that weight available. In some cases, the dog may have been rolled only once, but more often it has been several times, because that is the schooling process of a pit dog. Opinion varies on how often a young prospect should be rolled. Fanciers who have large kennels of dogs can keep a dog around just for schooling the pups. But even against a dog that is not too rough, a young dog may break or lose a tooth. (Incidentally, a Bulldog doesn't seem to suffer from such a trauma, the very same thing that would incapacitate a normal human being!) So one school of thought holds that the fewer rolls the better; if a dog is going to break a tooth, better that it happen in a match and not end his career before it gets started. Another line of thought believes that a pit dog learns a lot in each roll, and, for that

reason, the risk of breaking a tooth is worth taking to give the pup the experience he needs. Many are mindful of George Armitage's admonition that every fight takes something out of a dog. However, many would argue that those are only the long fights, going well over the half-hour mark.

Whatever the case, once the dog is open to match, the affair is consummated when someone else lets the owner know he has a dog at that weight. Forfeits are posted with someone, and contracts may or may not be drawn up. After all, they would have no legal standing, in view of the fact that they involve the particulars of an illegal sport. Their only purpose is to make it clear in the minds of both owners what the weight is and what variation of rules is to be used.

Once all the agreements have been made, a dog is put into a "keep," a system of exercise and feeding regimens. The pit-dog man may utilize the treadmill, flirtpole, swim tank, roadwork, or any combination of these. The training period may last for six to twelve weeks, depending upon the amount of money that is put up. The normal procedure is to post a forfeit amount, with the match purse being two and a half times as much, on the average. So, even if a pit-dog man wins, he isn't making much money for the time that he puts in with the dog. The only real reason for the forfeits and the purse is to make sure the guy conditions his dog and shows.

At match time, most dog men go through an agony of nervous apprehension as though they themselves were about to undergo the contest. It is not because of the money; rather, it is because they want their dogs to turn out well. They have invested considerable time in the dog, and they would be less than human not to become attached to the animal, and, of course, they want him to do well.

At the meeting place, a coin is tossed. The winner of the toss gets a choice as to whether to wash first or last. He generally picks first, so that the opponent's dog has to wait in the pit while his own dog is being washed. Much has been made of the washing ceremony by the humaniacs, usually prefaced with something like, "Dog-fighters apparently don't trust each other much, so they wash each other's dogs to make sure the other one hasn't put poison on his." True enough, but aren't there safeguards in all sports? It is only human nature that there will be some individuals to whom winning at any cost is the goal, even if it involves cheating.

Actually, most "rubs" that have been used on dogs in the past were designed to deter a dog from a favorite hold and, thus put him at a disadvantage. Some scoundrels even tried to use a nicotine sulfate solution on their dog and then cover it with a spray of silastic silicon. It sounds terrible, but it doesn't work. First of all, any "doper" takes a chance of poisoning his own dog (not to mention being shunned from the dog game if he is found out). Second, if a handler can't wash it off with a good combination of detergents and

Two Bulldogs playing tug of war, Pita and brother Kato.

Nick's Bianca. Breeder, Bob Wise.

warm water, a dog is not going to be able to lick it off. Generally speaking, I think it is fair to say that cheating defeats the purpose of the pit-dog game: to find out who has the gamest and best dog. Hence, although talked about a lot, doping is actually a rare occurrence.

After the second dog is washed and dried, he is brought into the pit where the first dog is waiting with his handler. Both dogs, incidentally, were *carried* to the pit, normally wrapped in the towel they were dried with. And, rather than kick their dogs, as reported by the charlatans, the handlers hold their dogs closely and try to keep them as calm as possible. Most of the dogs have been rolled enough (and

Baby Barney keeping a watchful eye on the front stoop and the photographer.

perhaps even matched before) that they recognize the pit and begin looking for the other dog, tending to fill with excitement and anticipation. The challenge is not to try to excite the dogs, but rather to keep them calm. However, once the other dog arrives, the referee endeavors to get the match under way without delay, as the handlers almost invariably have two very excited canines to hold onto!

The referee asks both handlers if they are ready and, upon receiving assurances that they are, he orders the dogs released. The dogs normally come together with a bang. Usually there is only initial growling, if that, and the dogs are immediately in holds. Each dog is trying to attain his favorite hold and wrestle his opponent to the mat. In the course of a normal match, the lead changes place many times, with first one dog down and then the other. All this time the handlers are watching their dogs, occasionally talking to them, constantly monitoring their condition, and observing the dogs' mouths to make certain that there are no broken teeth or that the dog is not "fanged," that is that he hasn't driven a canine tooth through his own flews.

As mentioned before, most people are first impressed with how craftily the dogs fight. Then they are surprised by how little apparent damage is being done. There are no slit throats or disembowelments, and broken bones are rare. These are formidable animals, but they are tough and hard to hurt, too. In any case, it is not the bloodletting that

most people anticipate. The truth is that the casual observer would soon become bored. After all, these dogs don't even make any noise when they fight. And, as intense as they are, and enjoy it as they do, they don't seem to be really mad at each other.

To the true connoisseur, the interesting part starts when the dogs begin scratching. This happens when one of the dogs turns his head and shoulders away from his opponent. It may only be a maneuver for a hold, but either his or the opposing handler may ask the referee for a turn. Once called, the dogs must be

Champion Gideon, a renowned pit dog now retired at stud.

121

Sam and Tia. Owner, G. McCurdy.

handled when they are free of holds, and the dog upon whom the turn was called is the one designated to scratch first. After that, the dogs scratch in turn. Incidentally, breaking sticks are not used in the pit unless one handler has conceded the fight. Handles must be made when the dogs are free of holds. The only other exception for using breaking sticks is if one of the dogs is badly fanged and the referee can't undo it with a stick or pencil while the dogs are in holds. The referee can then order the dogs parted with breaking sticks and, after unfanging the dog, he orders the dogs faced four feet apart and then released. Imagine if you will how calm are these dogs and how docile is their nature toward humans that the handlers can be so close to them (but they may not touch either dog!) and that a stranger (the referee) can put his hand in or near the mouth with impunity. Doesn't this give the lie to the often-stated notion that the pit is the source of all the people-mean dogs?

Anyway, the scratching is when the real devotee's interest perks up. (In fact, I recall with amusement one fancier saying that if there was a chorus line of the most gorgeous girls in the world on one side and a pit dog scratching on the other, he would be watching the Bulldog scratching. Such an attitude is a little extreme!) One reason for the interest is that the scratches are often spectacular in themselves. There is more to it than that. The match is most likely to be won or lost when one dog fails to scratch in the ten seconds he has to cross the pit and make contact with his opponent. So each time the dogs are picked up, it is the moment of truth for the scratching dog. Will he rush right back in the teeth of the fight even if he has been on the losing end of things up to this point? A dog that is taking a beating but scratches back repeatedly with enthusiasm always has the heart of the crowd.

Most matches last about forty-five minutes, usually ending when a dog fails to scratch or when his handler picks him up, for to continue will endanger his life beyond acceptability. If a dog does fail to scratch, it means he is not deeply game and, for that reason, not a prospect for either breeding or using as a match prospect again. I'm telling the truth about the game, as I am about everything else, so I'll tell you that most fanciers euthanize (destroy) such an animal. Usually it is done in the privacy of a camper or perhaps even later when the dog arrives home. The idea of doing it right away is to alleviate any unnecessary suffering on the dog's part. It most assuredly is not done for the purpose of the handler's disassociating himself from a loser.

Contrary to popular belief, Bulldogs make excellent pets.

But, let's face it, it certainly does seem like a brutal thing to put down a dog that has just shown more courage than any human ever would or could. It certainly is not a pleasant thing to do. However, good homes for any dog are hard to come by. Animal control centers that euthanize thousands of dogs daily can attest to that. In my opinion: Better a certain fate of peace than neglect. I believe that, so I don't

A puppy down from Old Family Red Nose breeding. Owners, George and Patte Owens.

Barney sneaks into forbidden bed.

condemn pit-dog men—or animal control centers.

In any selective breeding program, the theory is to raise up more dogs than you are going to use for breeding, and to select the very best for breeding. The problem has always been what to do with the ones that don't quite make the grade. The answer in the past was to sometimes find homes for the animals. But today, with the overpopulation of dogs—the solution has been to euthanize the culls. This is true in all dog games, not just the pit-dog game. Sled dogs have received much favorable publicity lately, and I have enjoyed it, because I like sled dogs (but not as much—alas!—as Bulldogs). However, I have seen sled dog people at work—good people. But after they are deep into the competitive aspects of their hobby, a dog had better not leave slack in the line and loaf when he should be pulling. This is true in all competitive breeding of dogs— including show dogs. In the case of show dogs, non-competitive stock can be sold as "pet quality" pups— sometimes! But there is plenty of euthanasia that takes place in this field, too.

Some would argue that at least it is

not a life-or-death competition with other dog activities. Well, really it is not supposed to be in the pit-dog game either. But, of course, because of its nature, it is more hazardous than most. But it is a simple matter of degree. I am told by knowledgeable Sheepdog people that those working dogs have an average life span of three years because so many of them are killed by the stock they work. Hounds are often lost on hunts, both to the quarry and just plain lost and never seen again. Retrievers drown and get killed working in water that has been sprayed with pesticides. Gun dogs get bitten by rattlesnakes. There is simply no safe path for any performance dog—not for any dog really. And not for people either.

The pit-dog game is a rough one. Dogs do get hurt. And some of them—very rarely—get killed in the pit. More often some die after a contest. Still, the game as bad as it is—and it most assuredly is not as bad as most people think!—has produced what almost anyone who has been associated with a Bulldog will attest is the best of dogs.

Sir Winston.

Arsuffis Mink, a two-time best of show (conformation) winner.

Above: William's Reuben, inbred Hyde's Satch and Bloody Sunday bloodlines, is the sire of several outstanding pit dogs. *Below:* Heinzl's Timex, as Heinzl said, a watch dog!

127

Above: Rhino, by Buck out of Dina-Mite, is 12 months old in this photo. *Opposite:* Barney visits brother Colonel K.

A Matter of Size

"The bigger they are the
harder they fall."
BOB FITZSIMMONS

"Fortune favors the
audacious."
ERASMUS

"But they always fall on me! "
HOWARD HEINZL

A newcomer to the breed is nearly always—as I was myself once—somewhat dismayed at the predominance of small dogs among the breed. After all, these are fighting dogs, so shouldn't they be huge so that they can dispatch other canines at will? Yet, the closer we get to pure pit stock, the more likely we are to have dogs that tend to be small. Can it be that size means nothing with these dogs? Such is not the case, for pit-dog men match exactly to weight and there is an art to bringing the dog in as close to the top weight as possible without exceeding it. If a dog goes uphill in

weight by even two pounds to win, he receives the approbation of pit-dog men generally, especially if he is going up against a good opponent.

Well, why this predilection for small dogs then? It is not a matter of trying to glorify the smaller man, for many of the pit-dog men who most preferred small dogs, such as W. R. Lightner, Bert Clouse, and Ham Morris, were extremely big men.

One theory, once advanced by Bert Sorrells, is that breeding good dogs is such a complicated business that by the time a fellow learns how to do it right, he is too old to handle large dogs, so he tends to prefer

Mims's Carolina Betsy, a granddaughter of Snooty and Bolio. Owner, Judy Mims.

small dogs. The idea merits consideration. And it is certainly true that there are many more good small dogs than there are big ones. However, even a poor, big Bulldog can usually whip a good smaller one. Anyway, there are some big dogs, rare as they may be, that are excellent pit dogs. Examples would be Colby's Pinscher, Burton's Hank, The Plumber's Alligator, and Powell and Wilkerson's Little Boots, to mention just a few that come to mind.

I have found that if you ask some of the big men I've mentioned why they prefer small dogs, they simply say that they are easier to work and cheaper to feed. But there lurks, in the back of your mind, the feeling that the answer is too simplistic, and it can't be the entire story. Isn't a big dog worth having simply because if he is the best at what he does, he is a candidate for the very best fighting dog in the world and not just the best at a given weight? True enough, but here is the rub. No one knows who the very top fighting dog is in the entire world regardless of weight, but I suspect that all but the most experienced pit-dog men would be surprised at what the weight of the dog was. I suspect that it would be between sixty and seventy pounds at pit weight. Bigger Bulldogs than that rarely come from quality strains. And even those of the size I've mentioned are rare—in quality especially.

As mentioned before, dogs smaller than sixty pounds have beaten Bandogges and Tosas with regularity. There are descendants of the old-time Bulldogs in Spain called *"Canario Presas,"* and I understand they are tougher than any of the other big dogs. They weigh about a hundred and twenty pounds; however, they, too, have fallen to quality American Pit Bull Terriers in the fifty- to sixty-pound range.

Also, as mentioned before, even small Bulldogs have beaten cur dogs (non-Bulldogs) and even the Bandogges. How can such a thing be? Size equals power. There is no denying that. The lions and tigers rule the cats, and they themselves don't attack elephants. The white shark rules the seas except for the killer whale, who is even bigger.

Henry's Ben.

Does the Bulldog stand as an exception to the general rule? Well, not entirely, for we would not expect him to subdue Siberian Tigers or elephants. However, he can subdue huge, behemoth bulls and wild boars. That is impressive enough. In fact, it is plenty impressive that he reigns supreme among canines irrespective of size. What I think is ignominious try at it but failed miserably. And back in the days that professional wrestling was a legitimate sport, Frank Gotch reigned as champion at a little over a hundred and eighty pounds and about five foot ten inches tall. (And he was generally considered the greatest of heavyweight champions.)

Now, returning to Bulldogs, we

Above: **Mims's Barney with a leg hold on Mims's Cora. Owner, Matt White.** *Opposite:* **Spartacus Champion Tuffy.**

operating here is that there just may be a natural size for dogs, a size that if he exceeds it, physical gains due to size begin to diminish. That size just may be somewhere around sixty pounds pit weight. It is only a theory to try to account for the phenomenon, but I'll assert it for now until someone comes up with a better one.

A similar size limitation in regard to fighting seems to exist among humans, too. We don't see any huge football players or basketball players becoming heavyweight boxers. Ed "Too Tall" Jones made an may wonder why a pit-dog man would be content to have thirty-five-pound Bulldogs that most assuredly are not in contention for the best in the world at unrestricted weight. However, they are candidates for the best at their weight, and that is good enough for our dog men. And there is no worry that such dogs would be bested by any big dog that wasn't just a bigger, better Bulldog (with occasional rare exceptions). These dogs are able to whip other breeds because their intensity and love for battle terrifies the vast majority of them, to the degree that they are

Left: Nicolas Accorti with Vashtie. *Below:* Riptide Pogo, descended from some of the best pit dogs, is a wonderful family pet shown here with a first-place trophy he won in obedience competition.

Heinzl's Badger, down from Chili and Blind Ben.

whipped from the very beginning. And those that have the grit to stay and battle a few moments are eventually worn down by the superior endurance and toughness of the smaller dog. And this goes without mentioning the craftiness that has been bequeathed from countless generations of the best of canine gladiators.

So the point is, even a small Bulldog can whip the general lot of curs; and, in bygone days, at least, he had the sympathy of the crowd in doing it, since his small size made him the "underdog." People could do no less than to marvel at how a little dog could best a big one, usually with considerable dispatch. And since even a small dog can be a fighter of no small ability, it is easy for us to comprehend how a small dog would be preferred, for, everything else being equal, a small dog is to be preferred for the sake of convenience in a number of ways (and they eat less). Of course, we give up the "image" of physical power with the small dog. But with most dog men, this is unimportant. If they

Maska's Georgia, a daughter of Triple S Champion Buster. Owner, Matt White.

Heinzl's D.B., a littermate to Hogan. Owner, Martin Street.

know in their heart that their little Bulldogs can whip any number of Great Danes or Mastiffs that may bark at them, it matters little to them if other people are blissfully unaware of the situation.

It might be of interest to ask if this is a situation isolated with dogs, one in which a small one can whip the rest of the lot. Can it have a parallel among humans? Yes, it can. And it does in two ways. One is if the human has become a really fine athlete in one of the combative sports. A small but skilled wrestler or boxer or martial arts specialist would have a decided advantage over larger but untrained men. I speak with more authority from the perspective of boxers and wrestlers, as I have done both of these. I have no experience with the martial arts, and I tend to be somewhat skeptical of them. The other way is that occasionally there are humans who are just born fighters in the sense that they have the knack for it. I knew of at least two such fellows when I was in the military. They were not trained in either boxing or wrestling, but they could scrap. Many a big fellow made the mistake of running afoul of one of these two. They simply had a natural ability for fighting. Now, of course, all of these smaller fellows could have been whipped by bigger fighters in their same class. The "born fighters" could have been whipped by bigger men who were also "born fighters." The wrestlers and boxers could be bested by larger wrestlers and boxers who have similar ability but have the advantage of size. But that is the way it is with the dogs, too. A small Bulldog can look like a million dollars whipping a big dog, but if he goes up against a decent and larger Bulldog, he is probably headed into his last fight. But, if the small Bulldog is a "real one," we can rest assured that the big one will not escape lightly.

Above: Bo Dragon's Tung, a 75-pound dog. *Opposite:* Hobo, by Heinzl's Gringo ex Chauvin's Victory, owned by Sara Chapman.

The Building Blocks of the Legend

"The American Pit Bull Terrier can do anything any other dog can do and then whip him as well."

JOHN P. COLBY

Strictly speaking, the Bulldog can't do everything that some breeds can do, but I know what old "J.P." meant. A Bulldog can't run as fast as a Greyhound or follow a trail like a scent hound. But one can sure make a good try at all these things, and some are better at it than others. I have already made mention of the American Pit Bull Terrier that won the Coonhound national field trial. And if you want a meat hunter instead of sport hunter, the Bulldog will be more likely to get you your coon. Being a still trailer (not giving

voice), he is upon the prey without warning like a thunderbolt out of the night.

But let's give the specialists their due. The Bulldog is not normally going to outdo them in their particular field. But he is so doggone adaptable and full of energy and curiosity and fun that he'll make a good try at just about anything.

The American Pit Bull Terrier's fighting prowess and clownish nature give rise to situations and stories that stick in the memory. No book of mine on Bulldogs would be

Ty's Cuervo, a son of Odom's Bad Bandit and Peyote of Portales. Owner, Ty Rains.

complete without including some of these stories. Some of the stories I know of firsthand, and others were told to me by men long dead, so I can't be certain of how true those particular ones are. But they have the ring of authenticity to anyone who knows Bulldogs.

A LION IN THE STREETS

Readers who have read my other books on the American Pit Bull Terrier will remember "Lion" from the stories told to me as a teenager by two businessmen in my old hometown in Colorado. I listened to the stories over and over again, never tiring of hearing them and always asking for details. Of course, I never dreamed that some day I would chronicle them. I just longed

to have dogs like Lion, Jocko, and Denver.

Lion was the big dog of the bunch, hence his name. It wasn't just because of his size either. He was colored like a lion, and his muscular head had the appearance of a lion's head. Further, he had been a kennel dog all his life and had only been used for fighting; and he was one of those Bulldogs that would attack any other animal: dog, cat, or dinosaur! So, although he would not be a danger to humans if he were loose (other than to induce a heart attack), he would, it was well understood, certainly wreak havoc among the animal population. For that reason, full precautions were taken to make sure the animal was secure.

However, Lion's owner, Ed, a man

of property and considerable influence, really liked dogs, and he wanted Lion to have as much freedom as good sense would allow. The burden of guilt from confining a dog was heavier in those days, as it was the general custom to allow all dogs to run free. (Bulldogs have always been, generally speaking, an exception to this rule. For that reason, they were known in Elizabethan times and earlier as "bandogs," which loosely translated means bound dogs or chain dogs.)

Ed had a cable system set up near an alley behind one of his businesses at which he was wont to spend considerable time. He could see the dog more often in that way, and Lion would get a little more attention, as employees soon learned that he was a friendly dog in spite of his formidable appearance. Passersby soon came to know Lion and greeted him, occasionally stopping to pet him.

The problem was that the handyman who put up the cable system was not as good at his job as Ed had been led to believe. Although he had had it impressed upon him about the great strength of the animal and how important it was that he not be allowed to get free, the man still did a slipshod job of putting up the cable. The most serious error was that the cable itself was not of sufficient strength; and perhaps the cable clamps were not tight enough. Whatever the case, it came to pass that one day Lion lunged at a passing cat, and suddenly he was free!

The first casualty was the cat. As

Hall's Champion Sugar is a four-time pit winner and a granddaughter of Hooten's Butcher Boy.

with other cats of the neighborhood, he had learned that Lion had limited range. Thus, Lion was upon him before he even tried to run away. It is extremely doubtful that the cat ever knew what happened to him. Lion shook the life out of him in an instant and flung the body to the top of the building. The dog indulged himself in a couple more cats he flushed out in the alley. A large Airedale, attracted by the commotion, seized one of the cats himself, only too happy to join in the killing orgy. What the Airedale didn't count upon was that Lion would drop the cat for larger prey in a second. Apparently, that is exactly what he did, for Ed's employees soon found the bodies of several cats and one of a large Airedale outside their boss's shop. Seeing that Lion had escaped but was no longer in sight, they reported that fact to the horrified Ed.

In telling the story, Ed, though he could laugh later on, said his mind immediately was filled with visions of Lion killing horses as he had the cats—and with equal ease. For this was back in the horse-and-buggy days, and there were countless carriages on the street, and even the milkman had a horse-drawn wagon. Just how much ill-will and money was this exploit of Lion's going to cost him? But, even with all those thoughts, Ed said his worst fear was that someone would shoot Lion.

As luck would have it, though, Lion didn't get any of the horses. After finishing off the Airedale, he ran down the alley and across some railroad tracks. On the other side of the tracks was a creek and beyond that a cow pasture. In the cow pasture were cows, sure enough, but there was also a large bull, one that insured that no one ever crossed that pasture. The bull probably saw Lion coming, and by the time the dog had

swum the creek and come over the fence, he was undoubtedly waiting there for him. He intended to send him on the run as he had all other dogs which dared to trespass on his ably defended grounds. He may have gotten his horns on Lion at least once, but, if he did, he didn't leave a mark on the dog. When the men found the two, Lion not only had the bull by the nose but had thrown him to the ground.

Ed had his men put ropes on the bull to hold him steady as he pried Lion loose with a breaking stick. Then he placed a harness on Lion and walked him back to the premises. Ed said that, as he walked Lion back, he noted with a combination of anger and amusement that Lion had not one mark on him and not one drop of blood. He looked as though he had merely been out for a walk in the park, and his tail wagged with satisfaction. He had enjoyed himself immensely!

BOZO AND THE MYSTERY OF THE RINGWORM

This story is of considerably more recent vintage. It involves a dog, bred down from Hooten's Butcher Boy, who was the first dog of the young fellow who acquired him. Thus he was raised as a house pet. He was what pit-dog men call a "hand-raised dog," and pit-dog men know that those are quite often the very best pit dogs. They have self-assurance; they are extremely cooperative; and they are invariably smart, something that seems to help them in the pit.

This dog turned out to be a tremendous pit dog. After winning two fights against other Bulldogs before he was two years old, he was turned over to an experienced pit-dog man for matching. It was agreed

Larry Bell with Bell's Lady Stomp.

that when the dog wasn't in training for a fight, the owner would get to keep him, and the owner would get him after his pit career was ended.

Well, our pit-dog man was absolutely astounded by this dog called Bozo for a number of reasons. For one thing, he had seen his last match, and he knew he was a formidable pit dog. He was well beyond the ordinary in the pit-dog category, as our dog man, whom we'll

in his eagerness to get to it. If he is loose, no command will stop him from taking the springpole. To Harry's astonishment, Bozo, even though he became as enamored of the springpole as most Bulldogs, would not attack it until told to do so. Further, he would hop up on the treadmill on command, but he would wait for word from Harry to begin running it. And he would run it at the speed Harry dictated, and he

Junior Jay Are. Courtesy of Humbolt Pit Bull Club.

call Harry (not his real name, of course), was of the opinion that he was a candidate for the best forty-eight-pound pit dog in the country. Aside from that, the dog was trained so well that he could be allowed to run loose and be trusted not to attack other dogs. (If they attacked him, that was their problem!) Further, he had not been trained to work the springpole or treadmill, but he learned very quickly.

Now, most Bulldogs become quite enamored of the springpole, and when they see one, they'll attack it just as they would another dog. If you have one on a lead and take him into a yard in which there is a springpole, he'll nearly pull you over

would stop on Harry's command.

To understand how remarkable this dog was, the reader must know that the majority of pit dogs are kennel dogs. (In pit-dog parlance, they might be more likely called chain dogs or yard dogs.) In any case, these dogs have been raised for fighting, so they are only taken off their chains to be worked or to be rolled. In either case, the enthusiasm of the dog is so great as to be maniacal. Even dogs raised as pets that learn to use a springpole or treadmill (or other such device) are hard to control in enthusiasm. Even pets have to be taken off the springpole with a breaking stick, for example. So Bozo's extreme

Right: Two Pit Bulls in Holland. On the left is Missy of Bolio breeding and on the right, Onklin's Schot Jr. *Below:* Martin's Rachael with Dean Martin.

Shebesta's Justice, by Champion Sooner out of Weldon's Miss Kitty, making Justice double-bred Jimmy Boots. Owner, Billy Stevens.

tractability was more than just a matter of his having been raised as a pet. He was a very unusual dog. But he worked so well and was such a pleasure to work with that when it came time for the match, Harry felt he had his dog in as good a condition as any dog he ever worked. This was good, for Bozo would need every advantage in going up against his opponent Swamper, a five-time winner and a devastating Bulldog.

In the match, conditioning was the main thing to decide the contest in Bozo's favor, as the Swamper dog had more talent in the sense that he held Bozo out and leaned on him, making him do all the work. He made him miss holds and gave him nothing to bite but air most of the time. Finally, after nearly half an hour, Bozo got his first real hold. In just another fifteen minutes, Swamper's handlers decided to pick the dog up to save him.

Once Bozo was all healed up, he was returned to his owner, as previously agreed upon. He went back to his carefree life as a house dog. Although he stayed in the house a good part of the time, he had a doghouse outside at which he spent his nights. One day, Bozo's owner brought the dog back to Harry with a problem. The dog had lesions in his skin and the owner wasn't sure what

Right: Champion Chino is a son of the great Shaft dog. *Below:* Nick's Brewzer enjoying the good life.

they were. Harry recognized the problem immediately as ringworm, a type of fungus infection given its name because of the worm-like lesion it leaves upon the skin.

Curing the ringworm was no problem, but Harry was puzzled. The dog had to contract the ringworm from some contaminated source. Harry questioned Bozo's owner. No, the dog had not been around any

only seven years old. (Since Bob is over eighty-five years old, I feel reasonably safe in asserting that he has had the longest experience with the dogs of anyone living!) A problem was that Bob's father raised Coonhounds and bird dogs for his hunting activities. When Bob received the puppy, neither he nor his father knew that this pup was of a fighting breed. Nevertheless, the

Stormy and Turbo playing together.

other dogs. He preferred the company of children, as he absolutely loved being with them; however, none of the children were likely to have given the dog the fungus. Finally, the problem was solved. It turned out that Bozo was letting the stray neighborhood cats share his doghouse with him on the cold winter nights!

ROWDY AND THE PAPER

Bob Wallace told me this story about one of his boyhood dogs. And perhaps the stage should be set.

You see, Bob was first given a Bulldog pup by his aunt when he was

pup soon became a favorite of the family. But when he grew old enough, he nearly killed one of the hunting dogs that had tried to bully him, so he was very quickly relegated to a kennel by Bob's father.

The pup had lived up to his name of Rowdy, and, yet, he wasn't really rowdy, being, like most Pit Bulls, rather mild of manner when not confronted by another canine. Although he had been raised as a house dog, he eventually accepted life in the kennel philosophically, but his most treasured times were the evenings when he would bring in

A Bulldog exported from the United States to Germany.

the paper and, as a reward, he got to spend time in the house before being put back out in the kennel.

There came a time that Bob's father had a new Setter pup, and he, too, got to receive time on the porch, later to be let in with Rowdy, so that the pup could receive a little extra attention, which Bob's father believed (quite rightly) a pup needed. But when the paper was delivered through the slot in the closed-in porch, the pup attacked it with glee and tore it into countless pieces. That meant that Rowdy had no paper to bring in. Worse yet,

Rowdy didn't get brought in at all because no one was sure that he hadn't joined in with the pup in such unseemly and destructive play.

This happened two more times. We can only imagine the horror of Rowdy, as he observed his ticket into the house being destroyed nightly. It is not in the nature of a typical Pit Bull to harm a pup in any way. For that reason, Rowdy was, no doubt, in a quandary. But he finally solved the problem!

On the fourth night, Bob's father came out to the porch, hoping to be early enough to rescue the paper.

Brandt's Josie Wales pulling for bait; Butch Slater holding the hide for bait.

Colby's Bud was, as Louis Colby said, "a good-natured slob but with a big motor inside."

There was nothing there. No newspaper. No shreds of paper carpeting the wooden floor, as had been the case the three previous nights. Rowdy, wagging his tail a mile a minute and obviously pleased with himself, trotted over to the porch swing, leaped upon it, and, with his paws on the back of the porch swing, reached high up into a cubbyhole in the brick wall and pulled out the paper.

Now here was a case that would impress even an expert on canine behavior (that is, a legitimate expert, such as a cynologist or ethologist—not just any dog trainer). A certain amount of reasoning had to go into the idea of grabbing the paper before the pup could get it and then placing it out of his reach in order to protect it. And the behavior did not go unrewarded, as Rowdy was not only brought in but received an extra treat and high praise for his ingenuity.

Later, however, he demonstrated that dogs, even smart ones, are slaves to habit—even more so than we humans! For after the pup was

Right: St. Benedict's Cher Cher La Femme, a grandson of Boomerang. *Below:* Schiller's Queenie.

151

SEGMENT# THE BUILDING BLOCKS OF THE LEGEND

A Bulldog playing frisbee with his master.

grown to the point that he was either sold or put in the kennels, Rowdy continued to put the paper in a safe place when it arrived, just as he had been doing all those months preceding the pup's absence. If Rowdy could have talked, perhaps he would have rationalized his behavior. It was not habit at all. It was just that a dog could never be too careful with a newspaper!

A SPOOK ON THE LOOSE

I have told elsewhere of my boyhood dog, Spook. Although I had other Bulldogs in my youth, he was the one that I had the longest, and he was a special companion that I took so many places with me. Here he was just an old kennel dog that had been converted into a house dog of sorts. (He spent the day on a chain and had a doghouse outside, but he got to come inside at night, and he slept in my room, near my bed.)

Unfortunately, there came a time when I was forced to part with him. I was about to graduate from high school, and I had plans of either going to college or entering the military. In either case, I wanted to find Spook a good home with someone who understood Bulldogs. I had been corresponding for some time with I.D. Cole of Phoenix, Arizona, and I wrote him, asking if he would be interested in the dog. (The dog men in Denver, as usual, were up to capacity with dogs.) In view of the fact that Spook was a Lightner dog and that that strain commanded more than a modicum of respect, I felt Cole might be interested in having him and that he would take good care of him.

Left: **Douglas's Champion Dirty Harry is owned by Mary L. Schaeffer.**

Opposite: **Jeff Burke and Mims's Mose. Carl Mims called him the gamest dog he'd ever bred.**

152

I well remember the day that I shipped old Spook off. Dogs were only shipped by train in those days, and Spook was in for a two-day trip. I recall my grandmother objecting to my shipping off the dog because he "worshipped" me so. But, what else was I to do? I couldn't take him to either college or the military with me, and my grandmother couldn't take him, as she had a dog of her own and had grown rather fond of it and knew what Spook would do to it. Anyway, putting that old brindle dog in that wooden crate was difficult for me. I gave him a farewell hug and slid down the wooden door. It never occurred to me to nail down the door. How would a dog ever raise a smooth sliding door that had no projections?

As I later learned from Cole, Spook arrived in good shape. He put the crate with the dog in it in his station wagon and stopped off at his office on the way home. Upon arriving home, he opened the back and was surprised at how lightly the crate slid out. Then he discovered the cause: the dog was no longer in it. As Cole said later, he never could figure out how Spook got the door up, but once out, he would have had no problem, as the windows had been left down in the car to protect the dog from heat build-up.

Upon discovering the loss, Cole contacted a judge-friend of his to keep an ear to the ground in regard to any dog incidents, and he placed a lost-dog advertisement in the paper. He knew that his insurance would cover whatever damages Spook did to other animals (actually, he was only a threat to other dogs, as he didn't bother with anything else); however, he was worried about Spook being hit by a car or getting in a fight and having a bunch of people beating on him with rocks, sticks, and clubs (as people are wont to do).

Finally, his newspaper advertisement bore fruit. A man called saying that before coming in to read the paper, he had just given water to a dog answering that description.

Cole immediately jumped into his car and drove to the area. He drove around aimlessly in the neighborhood in which Spook had been spotted, but he saw nothing. Just as he was ready to give up, he spotted him. He was walking along the sidewalk, apparently trying to get his bearings to try to find home. Cole parked the car and approached

Spook, calling him by name. Spook wagged his tail and approached, but when Cole tried to take hold of him, Spook moved off, keeping a couple of arm lengths away. Now, Spook was by no means a shy dog, but he apparently was not about to let anyone stop him in his search for home. (Tears came to my eyes as I read Cole's account of all this later, and even now it affects me to tell the story.)

Spook moved on up the road, and Cole followed him in his car, stopping at various intervals to try to get Spook in the car or to get a hand on him, all to no avail. Finally, the car overheated, and Cole was on foot following the dog. He said later that it wasn't long before his tongue was hanging out longer than Spook's. When a dog would come charging out at Spook, he became a statue, with head and tail up, staring holes through the dog. Although Spook was only a forty-three pound dog, there wasn't a dog large or small that didn't back off from that ominous brindle dog.

Finally, Cole came to the realization that the only way to catch Spook would be to get a dog on him. So the first pay phone he passed (for

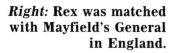

Above: Jessica and John Wayne, a merle-colored Pit Bull, a very odd color for a Bulldog.

Right: Rex was matched with Mayfield's General in England.

A very solid, solid-black dog on a field.

they were now in the heart of Phoenix), he called a dog man, explaining the problem. A posse of dog men was organized, and a dog named Spike was selected as a catch dog for Spook. (This Spike, incidentally, was destined to be an ancestor of Dibo. Another interesting tidbit was that Howard Heinzl, Wiz Hubbard, and Leo White were among the men who made themselves available to help corral Spook.)

In the meantime, Spook was continuing into the heart of Phoenix with Cole about a half a block behind. The first car to spot the dog alerted the others, and they made plans to converge at the next intersection. Three cars came screeching up to the intersection just as Spook reached it, and Spike was released from one of the cars.

Like a guided missile, Spike sped straight into Spook. The two dogs grappled for an instant. Then they were converged upon by a group of men who separated the animals with breaking sticks. Each dog was whisked into a separate car, and Cole came running out of nowhere to jump into one of them. The cars then proceeded to speed off in opposite directions. All of this happened in front of a large downtown crowd.

Some of them today may still be wondering just what it was that they saw that day!

THE BULLDOG TRAP

In all my years of Bulldogs, I have never stopped questioning if I have lost perspective. Could it be possible that I am wrong and everyone else is right? I am not entirely without conscience, and I do love animals, particularly dogs, and I would be heartsore to learn some day that I had a blind spot that kept me from seeing that Bulldogs are an unworthy breed, as some of the humaniacs assert, and it would be best for them and the world that they become extinct. Further, could it be possible that cruelties abound in the activity of pit fighting, an activity that I not only fail to condemn but have been known to defend? I do all this soul searching, not just because I have my weak moments, but because I want to deliberately re-evaluate all my ideas about these

dogs. I don't want to end up bullheadedly sticking to opinions that not only are wrong but are harmful.

A phenomenon that I have seen occur again and again has helped make me feel that I may not be so far off base after all. I have known many a man who absolutely condemned the idea of matching dogs and ended up an absolute fanatic at doing so himself. One such man was a Staf fancier who called me up years ago denouncing my attitude about Stafs (whatever that is!). I was patient with the man, for I was impressed by his intelligence and knowledge (for a

This Bulldog obviously feels that a Mack truck should have a *real* Bulldog for a hood ornament.

Yang with Mary and Elton III.

show-dog person!). However, I certainly didn't change his mind about the cruelty and immorality of pit contests. But something did! For years later, he became an extremely active matcher of dogs, and he was an absolute expert on the pedigrees of all the pit dogs in the country. If I ever needed to know anything about the real breeding of a particular dog, he was one of the best sources to contact for a real credible and carefully researched opinion.

The above is just one of many examples, and I'm not quite sure what sucks these people into the pit-dog game, other than the charm and fascination of the dogs. For it is a fascination that is felt, to some degree at least, by everyone. But

A brindle and white example of the breed waits patiently while his owner takes a break from their walk.

Austin's Punky Face, courtesy of Humbolt Pit Bull Club.

there are many ways to get "Bulldog fever" without even being aware that it is happening to you. The following example will suffice to illustrate the point.

A man we'll call Chuck (not his real name) was a professor of agriculture at a well-known college. He was also a breeder of exotic cattle, and he owned a vast ranch for the purpose of raising these animals. In some of his experimental crosses, he used pretty rough bulls. One of the problems he was having was in finding stock dogs that could stand up to them. This problem led Chuck to becoming a minor authority on stock dogs, too, as he was determined to find a breed of dog that could handle his cattle. He worked with different types of Border Collies, all to no avail. There

is little doubt that the Border Collie is probably the finest all-around stock dog in the world and is indubitably the finest sheep dog. However, none of these dogs could handle Chuck's cattle. The same turned out to be true with the Kelpie, the Queensland Heeler, and a number of lesser lights.

It was not until Chuck had received a full understanding of just how difficult a problem he had that it was solved. He discovered the American Pit Bull Terrier. Actually, the first dogs he discovered were possibly crossbred dogs, but they led him to the purebred Bulldogs, and he eventually decided that the purebreds couldn't be beat for stock work. I well recall Chuck's father expressing his amazement about how one of those little forty-five-pound dogs could completely subdue one of those behemoth steers, usually by seizing him by the nose and throwing him as he tried to run away. So it was that Chuck became interested in the breeding and genetics of catch dogs. One thing led to another as he wondered about the origins of such unbelievable ability and such awesome courage. He began to study the lines of fighting dogs. Eventually he began to build

his own fighting line and to match them himself. He had been taken unawares, and he was hooked.

Not only was Chuck heavily infected with the fever, but his comely wife became even more fascinated by the dogs than Chuck, if such a thing was possible, and she became an authority in her own right.

I had the pleasure of visiting Chuck's farm (which we would have

A Dutch-bred dog down from Greenwood's Scarlet. Owner, Bob Bock.

called a "ranch" in the West), and I had taken with me my oldest son, who was a mere teenager at the time. Chuck's farm was so big that we went to see the dogs by truck, as the dogs were staked out in different areas all over the farm. Riding in back of the truck with my son was Casey Jones, who had driven us up to Chuck's place (as we were strangers in a strange land, a thousand miles away

TUDOR'S CHERRY WASHES OUT AS A HOUSE DOG

This story is one that was told by Bob Hennenberger in an old *Your Friend and Mine* magazine, and some readers may have seen the story. I don't have access to that particular issue now, so those old timers who do have the issue can check the accuracy of my memory for details. (Please be kind and take into

Bell's Baby Jones is a descendant of Bolio and Red Neck. Owner, Larry Bell.

from home and easily becoming lost on main thoroughfares and certainly in the backwoods of Chuck's territory). Casey was a successful attorney and a son of a state senator. I was feeling a little chagrined at having so august a person taking turns with my son at jumping off the back of the truck and opening gates as we went from one area of the spread to another. Chuck, apparently sensing my feelings as Casey was opening a gate, commented, "When Casey makes judge, we'll let him ride up front with us!"

account that it has been over thirty years since I've seen the story!)

For those who don't know, Mr. Hennenberger (whose name I may be misspelling) was a professional cartoonist as well as a Bulldog devotee; and he drew many quite funny cartoons in regard to Bulldogs for Pete Spark's use when he put out the magazine. Bob utilized drawings to illustrate his little story in this instance, and as I recall, Tudor's Cherry was a red, red-nosed bitch that had been raised on a chain by Earl Tudor. Hennenberger was

High Country Russ, a descendant of Going Light Barney. Owner, High Country Bulldogs.

A son of Hoover
out of a
daughter of
Peterbilt.

impressed by the bitch's intelligence, as she would entertain herself on the chain by playing with flowers and blades of grass. She seemed downright scholarly in the way she would take her paw and push a blade of tall grass down and then watch bemusedly as it would begin to right itself. There were other things that she would do, too, that impressed Bob with her intelligence.

In some way Bob gained possession of Cherry, and in view of her intelligence, he decided to try her as a house dog. Now, let us stop for a minute and think what it must be like to be raised as a pure pit dog, as such was the case with Cherry.

First, you are restrained to a rather small world, either a kennel run or, more likely, a chain, and not much happens in this restricted world. You occasionally get petted, and the high point of the day is feeding time. It is this aspect of breeding dogs, *any* breed of dogs, that I consider to be the most cruel because of the intelligent, affectionate, and social animals that dogs are. However, it is probably not as bad as outsiders might think, as the dogs know no other existence or, if they had, they soon become adjusted to it. It is surprising how even humans can become adjusted to almost any type of existence and even find happiness in a way of life that previously may have seemed intolerable to them. In the case of Bulldogs, though, they have a special desire to fight that wells up in them as they mature. Not being Bulldogs, it is difficult for us to conceive of the mentality that would take such joy in fighting. But then, it is also difficult for us to understand fully just why a Coonhound finds such joy in following a trail or a Border Collie in herding sheep.

In any case, about the only time a Bulldog is taken off the chain is

Accorti's Vashtie.

when it is to be rolled. (If he is of match quality, there will later come a time when he will be put in a keep, and he will be taken off the chain for various types of exercise activities which the dogs almost invariably come to love.) Since being taken off the chain is a treat in itself and the dogs have been bred for fighting and thus come to love it, it is not any wonder that as they get into the routine, they become quite excited when they are taken off the chain and always think they are going to be rolled. The excitement they demonstrate is enthusiastic and contagious. The other dogs, too, seem to know what is happening, and they raise all kinds of Cain in their excitement (and perhaps resentment in being left out of the fun!).

All this brings us to another point. Bulldogs are almost without exception extremely excited by seeing other dogs fight. They obviously know what is happening, and they seem to obtain a vicarious thrill out of it. However, they can be fooled. I presently have two brothers, Hoover and Isaac, who have remained friends but will occasionally playfight. But it looks like the real thing, and a human observer would be fooled. And it fools my other dogs too, as they raise all kinds of hell, and I have to tell them to knock it off! Now the reader may notice that I qualified what I said about Bulldogs becoming excited, as Howard Heinzl once had a Bulldog that could lie down outside the pit and take a nap while two dogs were fighting. And he was a game dog, too. My Dillinger Dog, felt by many to have demonstrated outstanding gameness in a two-hour match (before I got him), was of the same mold. However, it is an uncommon trait. More typical was the dog that Heinzl had who, when they rolled the dogs in a pit that wasn't far from where he was chained, would leap several feet in the air to grab onto a tree branch from which he hung and worked over while the dogs were fighting. Howard used to say that he got a better workout than the dogs in the pit!

Kitty the Bulldog and Barney taking in the street scene.

Nick's Admiral Kirk.

Above: Iron Jaws Mabies Buddy, a champion pit dog who is also an obedience competition winner. *Above right:* Doug Berben's Whizzer. *Right:* A hardy young Bulldog with demonstrated potential.

Anyway, here we have Bob Hennenberger ready to make a pet out of a bitch who has led the kind of life I have just described, a lifestyle that is most inclined to make a dog a "fight-crazy fool." (Is it any wonder that many pit-dog men are unaware of just how intelligent these dogs are and what good pets they make when all they have experienced are the fight-crazy lunatics who know no other existence?) Now, of course, this brings up a point: if the dogs are exposed to a life as a house pet, will they still be fighters? Yes, they will. In fact, they will be even better than they would have been otherwise, for

their intelligence has been allowed to reach its full potential, and there is something about being a house dog that gives a pit dog even more confidence in himself than he would have otherwise. Experienced pit-dog men would like to have all their stock "hand raised." Having discussed all this, can we pretty much guess the kind of experience Bob is going to have with Cherry?

Bob takes Cherry off the chain, and she thinks she is going to get to fight. She is excited, but she controls herself, to a degree at least. Bob puts her in his car. That's okay; Cherry has been in a car before—when she

Pogo with his pal.

Solis's Champion Brynner is a four-time pit winner.

was taken some place else to fight. Arriving at his house, Bob puts Cherry on the lead and walks her into the house. Again, this is not completely outside Cherry's experience, as she has been taken to indoor pits before. Once inside, things are still reasonably familiar, but there is no pit, no plywood walls about three feet high to make a sixteen-foot enclosed area. And there is no other dog, not even the smell of one. Cherry is plainly puzzled, but she is in the fight mode from past habits.

Bob, observing that Cherry is by no means cowed by the unfamiliar surroundings and is outwardly calm, removes the leash from her collar. (What Bob did not observe was that Cherry was eyeing an easy chair across the room.) Upon being released, Cherry scratched straight into the easy chair, boring into its soft underbelly, pushing it into a corner. We can imagine Cherry's contempt for such an "easy" opponent. Here she is getting no resistance at all, and she has her adversary already on its back, stuffing is coming out, and when she shakes out her hold, stuffing, wood reinforcement, and springs fly all over the room!

Soon Bob had hold of Cherry, carrying her away from her ruined opponent. It has been so little time before he got to her and yet so much damage! Bob gave up easily. That very day Cherry was back on her chain, content at another good day's work.

HOOVER AND THE BALL

Many years ago, I made a breeding of a double-bred daughter of Barney to Champion Little Boots, a son of Grand Champion Hank. The breeding was made for the purpose of obtaining females for my own use. Instead, I got four males. Such are the frustrations of the breeder! In view of the fact that I had wanted females, I intended to sell the males, and I did sell two of them. However, my wife, who has an eye for dogs, took a particular shine to Hoover, as she felt he was unusually intelligent and everything that a Bulldog should be. Well, if I were going to keep one pup, I decided why not keep the other too for the time being so that they would be company for each other in the puppy pen. The other pup we called Isaac (in my mind he was being named after Isaac Newton or Isaac Asimov, but my friend Jim Isaac thought that it was being named after him and kept saying, "That dog had better not quit!").

It became part of my routine to let the puppies out and play ball with them. Hoover really took to the ball playing bit. Isaac loved to play, too, but, as one of my sons said, "Isaac just does it because Hoover does." Actually, I think that Isaac would have been a ball dog even without Hoover, but his performance, good as it was, paled beside Hoover's adroit ball handling and unreal enthusiasm. Both dogs got so they could track a ball extremely well in

The author throwing the ball for Hoover while Isaac waits his turn. Unlike most other Bulldog males, Hoover and Isaac get along, and, contrary to common opinion, that doesn't mean that they aren't game.

Above: Riptide Hoover retrieving a ball which the author has thrown. *Below:* Tank.

the air and catch it without letting it bounce. Also, both dogs would swim to the bottom of a swimming pool in order to retrieve the ball. (I was using the heavy density balls with extra bounce built in.)

At the age of two years, Hoover and Isaac were in the same puppy pen and were fed together without any growling, let alone outright fighting. Other dog men couldn't believe it. I simply told them that I gave my Bulldogs a proper upbringing and they only fought if I gave them permission. No one said anything, but I'm sure that some questioned my judgment about the kind of Bulldogs I kept. I was unworried. My experience had been that the easygoing Bulldogs were sometimes your best ones.

One day my wife, Stephanie, came running to get me because Hoover and Isaac were fighting. My son and I separated the two dogs and, later, when the dogs had cooled off, we were able to put them back together again, and they got along fine. We had no idea what had touched them off, and I was violating a cardinal rule of my own: never let two grown Bulldogs stay together unsupervised. Besides that, I was not a little concerned about Hoover. You see, Isaac didn't have a mark on him, and when we came upon the dogs, Isaac was holding Hoover out by the ear, and all Hoover was doing was barking. The inability to get to Isaac didn't bother me. The barking did. In my experience, the quiet fighting Bulldogs are the best. The noisemakers are generally suspect. A few weeks later, though, John and I had another occasion to separate the two dogs. It was in a blinding rainstorm. Hoover had gotten to Isaac this time, and both dogs were fighting silently. Hoover had Isaac by the shoulder, and he was lifting him high in the air and slamming

him down into the ground. There were a number of mud puddles in the pen, and it seemed that Hoover had doused Isaac in each one! It was a real chore getting these two powerful animals apart as we slipped around on the slick mud. This time Hoover went to a kennel run of his own. The two dogs get along fine to this day under supervision, but we don't leave them together unsupervised any longer. I'm taking my own advice.

We, of course, had no idea what may have started the animals' fighting. I have a theory that, whatever it was, Isaac was the aggressor. Hoover's barking on the previous occasion was partly out of bafflement that his good buddy would attack him.

Stephanie's instincts, as usual, were unfailing, as Hoover had matured into a remarkable Bulldog, a good-looking dog and an extremely intelligent one. I had to keep a bolt in his kennel latch, as he had figured out how to open it. It is difficult to convey how intelligent this animal is—almost as difficult to convey as his enthusiasm for playing ball. Once, at the beach, I threw his ball farther out than I had intended. It was murky water that day, and, of course, Hoover couldn't use his nose under water. I was amazed how long he could hold his breath as he swam head down, feeling for the ball, with only the tip of his tail sticking up out of the water. Other swimmers began to panic. One girl waded toward him, saying, "That dog! That dog!" She apparently felt that he was drowning from something, perhaps something had hold of him and was pulling him down head first. We explained he was just looking for his ball, and finally he came up with it. Everyone was dumbfounded. I think determination sparked by his great appreciation of the challenges of

Riptide Isaac, a brother to Hoover, is shown here making a beeline for a thrown ball. Owner, Dick Stratton.

Buck, an English dog, is down from Stubblefield's Buddy.

finding the ball enabled him to stay under so long.

Readers of my book *The World of the American Pit Bull Terrier* may recall the story about the ball playing of my house dog Becky. Both Hoover and I wound up in the doghouse over her death. You see, one of the ways that Hoover demonstrated his intelligence was that he could open his kennel latch and all the other dogs', too. Although I nearly always remembered to put the bolt in Hoover's latch to his kennel run, I forgot to do it one day. Hoover apparently discovered the latch was off some time during the day while we were gone. In recreating the incident based on the evidence, I assert that Becky apparently found Hoover loose out back and jumped him. I know she had to continually push the fight, as Hoover is unbelievably mellow, and he is especially reluctant to fight females. My family came home before me to find Becky dead and Hoover and Isaac loose.

I thought about trying to shift the blame from Hoover onto Isaac, but I could see that such a tactic was hopeless. Blood was on Isaac's gatepost and latch, so Hoover had committed the foul deed and afterwards let Isaac out to play with him—completely conscienceless about what he had done to Becky!

Although I tell the story in a light-hearted way and in a rather flippant manner, we were devastated by the loss of Becky, as she had been our house dog for some time, and she was the last of our relatively pure Wallace dogs. She was full of

Bell's Pinky Jones. Owner, Larry Bell.

personality and was loved, not only by the family but by many of our friends, too—many of them non-dog people. The main thing that kept Stephanie and the rest of the family from blaming Hoover was their knowing the dog; everyone knew that Becky had to keep pushing the fight, even unto her own death.

Hoover proved to be relatively game later on in an accidental kennel fight with an extremely rough dog. I mention this only because it is important to keep in mind as I tell the next part of the story.

As I said before, Isaac and Hoover were never together unsupervised after their second fight. However, they did have a third fight that took place when they were running together as part of my clean-up routine. I always did, and still do, let them run together while I clean the kennel runs and the areas of the other dogs. After cleaning up, I put the equipment away, and spend some time playing ball with the two

Below: **Boots McCoy. Owner, Pat Chilton.**

brothers. Only this time, something had touched off a fight. I remember only dimly what it was. I think I had a new and aggressive female in the yard, and she was challenging Isaac through the fence. Isaac was responding to some degree, Hoover was ignoring the entire thing; but he was in a playful mood and jumped Isaac for one of their rounds of roughhousing. Isaac was in the fight mode and grabbed Hoover by the ear, and, before long, they were locked in combat.

I was alone at home at the time. I had no help to part the two fighting animals. One way to do it would be to get a collar and leash on one of them, tying him to a fence or a tree. It would still be tricky, but I could then eventually get the two dogs apart with skillful use of the breaking stick. But I had another idea. Knowing how ball-happy Hoover was and how he really didn't want to fight his old friend Isaac, I tried something. Hoover had Isaac down on the ground by the shoulder, shaking him brutally. I got his ball and rolled it right in front of him, directly across the gaze of his eyes, which were presently locked in murderous concentration on Isaac. No response the first time, but the second time I did it, his eyes tracked the ball for a second. The third time, I rolled the ball so that it would stop in his view, then I picked it up and threw it. Hoover dropped Isaac and flew after the ball. I deftly laid hold of Isaac, who was flying right back at Hoover, and I closed the gate of the pen in which they had ended up, as luck would have it, when they were fighting.

I had done it. I got two good dogs apart all by myself without a breaking stick. Only, I wasn't sure if I should tell other dog men about it. I did though. And those who knew Hoover laughed themselves silly and

didn't think anything less of the dog for it. For Hoover is different from other Bulldogs in one respect: there is one thing he likes better than fighting!

Rosso's Joe D asking "Is it soup yet?" Doberman in the background.

JOCKO IN THE SLAMMER

Readers of my other books on the American Pit Bull Terrier will recall Jocko as one of the dogs that I had heard about on numerous occasions from two businessmen who lived in my hometown. Both men are long dead and for that very reason, I am reluctant to give their full names. You see, I don't know their sons and

St. Benedict's Cher swinging from a rope. Owners, Mike and Terry Walsh.

daughters or how they would feel to have their fathers revealed in a book as devotees of pit dogs. Let me just say this: the man I referred to as "Howard the boxer" in my other books was no ordinary boxer. He twice fought for world championships, once for the middleweight division and once for the welterweight championship. Those matches were the only ones he ever lost, and they were lost by decisions only, one of them a split decision. I personally saw old newspaper clippings in which Howard was described as having the greatest defensive skills of any boxer the game had ever known. Howard had also been a race car driver before he settled down to a business life as the owner of a restaurant. He was sort of an idol of mine when I was a kid, and I got to know him because he sponsored a boxing club for interested youngsters, of which I became a member.

There was a time, after his boxing career, when Howard served as business agent for active boxers and professional wrestlers. (The big difference was that in those days professional wrestling was a legitimate sport, and the wrestlers were phenomenal warriors.) It was during this time that Howard engaged in his hobby of matching dogs. He still had Jocko, or rather he had regained him to use as a match dog after his career as an active fighter was over. (I have told elsewhere how Jocko was a distraction to Howard's professional boxing career!)

Most people these days seem to feel that matching dogs was legal at one time. Such people are usually unaware that professional boxing and wrestling were themselves illegal not so long ago. And, while

there may have been no specific laws on the books against dogfighting, local authorities raided such activities regularly if they knew about them. Somehow, authorities found out about a clandestine meeting between Jocko and another twenty-eight pound pit dog in a warehouse in Denver. It was early on in the match, but Jocko was already ahead of his opponent when the alarm was sounded that the cops were busting in. The handlers hurriedly got their charges parted and took off running out another exit. Howard had been handling Jocko, and he was running down an alley, carrying Jocko under his trenchcoat. This was no mean task, as Jocko cared not one whit about the police, and he still had business to take care of back at the warehouse. He was not a passive passenger. In his struggles to free himself, he kicked loose the belt

Ibrahim Abdu sends his Chako's King up for some exercise.

Left: M and R's Butch, a very game half-brother to the great Jeep. *Below left:* Perry's Ms. Pacman, a great pit bitch.

Above right: STBs Dylan is a two-time winner and a son of Champion Peterbilt. *Right:* Greenwood's Scarlet.

from Howard's coat. The belt became entangled with Howard's legs, and down he went, head first into a pile of trash cans. Jocko was free.

To Howard's horror, Jocko headed straight back the alley toward the warehouse. At the entrance to the alley were the police in hot pursuit; at the sight of the hardcharging Jocko, they scattered like Keystone Cops, for they had no way of knowing that the intense little dog wasn't after *them*! Howard circled around and returned to the warehouse, in which he found Jocko sniffing around, looking for his obviously craven opponent who had apparently fled. Howard picked up Jocko, placed him once again under his coat, and tried to slip out of the darkened warehouse, but the police showed up and had their lights on him. He was caught at last.

Howard and his second for Jocko's match, an old friend from the fight game, were the only fish the police managed to net that night, and they placed all three, Howard, his friend, and Jocko, in a cell together. In spite

A Bulldog dressed by her owners, George and Patte Owens, to look "cool."

of the circumstances, they managed to get some sleep that night, even though they had no idea just how tough things might go for them. Howard had the most difficulty sleeping, as Jocko insisted on sharing his bunk and most definitely wanted his fair share of the room.

When morning came, Howard talked to the jailer about taking the dog out for a walk to empty out. The jailer contacted the precinct captain, who turned down the idea of Howard being allowed to take the dog out, but being a dog fancier himself, the captain offered to take Jocko for a walk. Howard gave the leash and collar to the officer, and Jocko led him down the hallway. Both Howard and his partner were amused at how the little dog surprised the captain with his strength and nearly pulled him off his feet. After that, the policeman maintained a tight grip on the lead and tried to walk with whatever dignity was possible with a twenty-eight-pound dog nearly pulling him over.

An alarming time passed, and when the captain returned, it was *sans* any pretense of dignity. He was in a rush. He had caked blood on his uniform, and Jocko was caked with blood, but he had his mouth open in a triumphant tongue-lolling grin, and he wagged his tail furiously, happy with himself and happy to see his two friends. The captain was a mixture of grudging admiration, mild anger, and sincere concern. "Take this hellion," he commanded, "Get out of here, and forget that you were ever here. Tell no one about it."

The two men were obviously delighted to be freed, but they couldn't resist asking what in the world had happened. "Well," the captain explained ruefully, "the mayor's German Shepherd is an awful bully. When he jumped this little dog, I thought he was going to kill him. But it wasn't him I should have worried about, even though he was on the bottom. That little dog killed that big dog from underneath. And all the time I was worrying about him! Not him I should have worried about. He's the devil himself, isn't he? Look at him wagging his tail, happy as an idiot—just pleased as punch with himself. Well, if you two gentlemen will excuse me, I have to go dispose of a body!"

And so it was that Jocko led even a minion of the law into disgraceful circumstances. But, in spite of that, according to Howard, not only did he become good friends with the captain, but the captain became a devotee of pit dogs.

Booger and Penny, the parents of Going Light Barney.

Above: **Fonseca's Jenny, a granddaughter of Fonseca's Pincher. Owner, Martin Street.** *Opposite:* **Su-Mesh and Boss. Su-Mesh is a descendant of Going Light Barney. Owner, Jesse Azure.**

Breeding Better Bulldogs

"*The greatest of faults, I should say, is to be conscious of none.*"

THOMAS CARLYLE

The first advice I would give about breeding Bulldogs is: don't do it! After all, it is much cheaper to buy a pup than to breed for that perfect dog. Keeping a number of dogs is a heavy responsibility. They must be taken care of, rain or shine and sick or well. It takes the sort of commitment that most people are not inclined to have—at least, no sane person! Further, it is useful to keep in mind that selling dogs to the general public is considered a vice in the rather bizarre world of pit-dog devotees. But, when you think about it, that particular attitude is not without foundation.

The situation now is that the American Pit Bull Terrier breed is under heavy siege, with some dim-bulb newspaper columnists and opportunistic politicians calling for it to be a felony to possess the breed. This is a hysteria, of course, but outrageous things are done during hysterias. In Scotland, four hundred years ago, because of an attack on one person by one Bulldog, by royal decree all mastiff-type dogs (the terms "Mastiff" and "Bulldog" seem to have been used somewhat synonymously then, and they may have referred to different sizes of the same breed, in some areas at some times) were taken from their owners and put to death. No wonder the importations to this country were primarily from England and Ireland!

We don't have royal decrees now of course in this country, but let's not kid ourselves. Some of the politicians we have had have been worse than any monarch. But the main point is that there is no basis for the hysteria that leads to outrageous legislation if the dogs are kept out of the hands of those who don't understand them and aren't committed to their welfare. Thus, it is best if these dogs are not sold to the general public. They are too good for most people anyway. So the condemnation of "peddlers" is not without warrant, and it has long been a tradition in this breed. For that reason, if you are going to breed Bulldogs, you need to know exactly where the pups will go—if you are a true friend to the breed. And all the homes must be suitable ones. With all the work that goes into it, there is little profit in breeding dogs anyway, and with taking special precautions, as custom dictates with this breed, the profit margin is, for all practical purposes, eliminated.

There are those poor souls among us, however, who find the greatest meaning in breeding their own dogs. In that way, when they come up with an exemplary specimen, not only can the breeders point with pride, but they can also see many of their past favorites in the progeny, as those dogs will be in the bloodlines of the newly bred animal.

Those who breed Bulldogs should be knowledgeable before they begin. It is better to study and learn ahead of time than to learn the hard way by picking it up as you go along—it is better for the dogs too. A major fault with breeders is in not being sufficiently selective. Some are blind to the faults of the breeding

stock, and some just make too many compromises for the purposes of saving a few dollars. If you can't afford a good bitch or the cost of a stud fee for an excellent dog, then save your money until you *can* afford it. You'll be off to a much better start, and you will not be digging your breeding program out of a hole all the time because of the poor original stock.

The question is, then, what constitutes a good Bulldog? In all my years with the dogs, I have found that the crummy dogs with unreliable dispositions have come from non-pit stock. Nearly all the great dogs, which were great pets and were useful for such things as hunting and stock work, came from pit stock. There is no doubt about it—the pit dogs are the class of the Bulldog world. It makes no difference how one feels personally about the morality of pitting dogs in a contest; the reality is that game dogs don't stay that way unless they are selectively bred for that trait.

That doesn't mean, of course, that a person has to be involved with dogfighting to breed good dogs. Many of the pit-dog men sell their best dogs when they are past their prime for matching, and they are bought by people who put them up to public stud. These, then, are the dogs to use as stud dogs. However, it will be necessary for you to do your homework to learn the history of the dog, who his ancestors are, and what their history is. It is only really

Opposite: **Heinzl's Hogan, a double-bred Heinzl's Blind Ben dog. Owner, Martin Street.**

necessary, though, to do this for three generations.

Before discussing breeding theory, let me briefly describe the ideal pit dog, since pit stock is associated with the best dogs we need to know the characteristics of the best dogs. What I am describing, it should be remembered, is in my opinion the *ideal* pit dog. To be sure,

any people-mean Bulldogs that didn't eventually quit. Of course, most pit-dog men would have culled out a people-mean dog the first time it showed that trait. One of the selective pressures that has produced such reliable dispositions in our dogs is that the dogs are often picked up in the pit and handled, and a propensity for a dog to snap or

Dunn's Clyde. Owner, Tim Dunn.

there have been some great pit dogs that varied in one respect or another from my description. But, if the reader can get an idea of the ideal pit dog, he can then envision the breed characteristics that make a good pet for a responsible owner. It will also help one to keep in mind just what it is that he is aiming for in his breeding program.

First of all, a pit dog is of a rock-steady disposition, cool under pressure and not the least bit snappy. Almost without fail, the good pit dogs have been of a completely mellow disposition with people, docile and friendly—even to strangers. The old-time dog men used to always claim that a people-mean dog was a cur. I never accept absolutes myself, but I can't think of

bite in these circumstances would be most undesirable.

An ideal pit dog has a strong desire to fight, and he enjoys fighting contact, but he keeps his head, even under the strong stimulus of a strange aggressive dog being in his presence. When I judge dog shows, I always have the handlers show me how the teeth mesh in the jaws of their animals. One of the reasons for this is to determine whether the dog has a scissors bite or not, but the other important factor is to find out for myself whether the owner can safely put his hand in his dog's mouth during a time that the dog is very excited because of other dogs' being around. I have never yet had a handler get bitten, and these show dogs are not highly bred pit dogs. I

Tucker with her owner Pat Wilson.

have had one or two dogs snap at the handler or me, and I have dismissed such dogs from the show, but that has been one or two dogs among the many thousands that I have judged. And, I have noticed, the dogs that I have known to be honest-to-goodness game pit dogs being shown were nearly invariably the calmest dogs of the lot. They liked to fight, sure, but they emanated self-confidence and friendliness toward humans and scarcely seemed to notice the other dogs—for what did they have to fear from them?

A good pit dog goes straight to his opponent and always moves forward. He keeps the pressure on, and snapping does not deter him. A good dog doesn't waste time sparring around but bores straight in, pressing for a good hold. But the point is, he stays in hold. If he can't get a good one, he'll take a bad one until he *can* get a good one. A holding dog is always at an advantage. Such a dog will neutralize a barnstorming dog by

Stevens's Pattie, by Charlie's Hoss Fly out of Champion Bessie, a blend of all three elements of the Stevens family of dogs.

Champion BJ from Bolio and Tonka bloodlines.

holding him out, making things more awkward for him. If he has the advantage, he works the hold to obtain even greater advantage.

A good pit dog has natural air and the intelligence to pace himself for a long fight. He is also tough to hurt and resistant to shock.

A good pit dog—in fact, nearly all of them—fights silently, not wasting precious breath on growling. Nor does he cry out; although the other dog's holds hurt, his enjoyment of the fighting contact overrides the pain. (Also, endorphins produced in the dog's brain help override pain.)

The ideal pit dog has an enthusiasm for working, whether it be running a treadmill, playing ball, working a springpole, or swimming in a swim tank. The enthusiasm is balanced by a nearly phlegmatic, easygoing attitude when he is in his pen or on the chain. Hyperkinetic (or "hyper") dogs have the disadvantage of always keeping themselves worn out and banged up.

I mention gameness last, but it is the most important trait. It means that neither fatigue nor pain nor the

psychology of being behind the entire time will cause the dog to lose his enthusiasm for fighting contact.

I have spent this time painting a picture of the perfect pit dog, since responsible breeders need an ideal to work toward. Although the *perfect* dog is theoretically impossible to achieve, the majority of the individuals in the breed can at least approximate the ideals—and produce worthwhile specimens. The enthusiasm for work carries over into life activities, such as playing ball or tug of war. Whatever activity you get your Bulldog involved in, he will develop such enthusiasm that he will often prevail even against specialists in that area. Thus, we have a Bulldog "blowing away" Greyhounds, shooting right past them to get to the lure. (It has happened, but even I would not predict that a Bulldog will outrace a racing Greyhound.) He will climb right up a tree to get a ball or a hide (or some other toy), and he will outswim, if he gets the chance to practice, water dogs such as retrievers and Newfoundlands. In

Above: Vashtie. *Left:* Riptide Bandit on the left and Riptide Rosie on the right are now residing in Malaysia.

Opposite: Moore and Street's Cosmo, a son of Clayton's Tadpole and a littermate of Grand Champion Art.

short, he will be a wonderful pet, always eager to participate in new activities, but he is not a hyper dog that will drive you crazy all the time. However, he is not a pet for everyone. But for those of us who are not willing to settle for anything less, there should be a certain appreciation of the fact that the dog is what he is because he has been bred for countless years for hunting and fighting.

THE MECHANICS OF HEREDITY

Strangely enough, it is not necessary to know any of what I'm about to cover in this section in order to become a successful breeder of Bulldogs. To be sure, the knowledge can be of some minimal help, but breeding is more art than science. Still, I remain convinced that Bulldog people should be better in every way than other dog people; we need to strive to be worthy of the dogs. For that reason, I am hoping to send some of you off to learning more about genetics by giving a

quick overview of what is known about the mechanics of heritability. Some of you, of course, already have this knowledge, and some others may want to skip this section anyway!

Through countless years of experimentation, scientists have discovered that transmission of both physical and mental traits are passed from generation to generation by genetic material (genes). Before that, it was widely believed that the blood was the vehicle for transmission of traits, and our language still shows traces of those beliefs. Thus, we speak of "bloodlines," "good blood," and talk of how "blood will tell." But actually it is the genes that carry the traits, and it is they which make up the long lines of chromosomes. Chromosomes occur in pairs in dogs and in humans, but the dog has more chromosomes than we do. We have forty-six chromosomes or twenty-three pairs, and the dog has seventy-eight chromosomes or thirty-nine pairs.

Not all organisms have paired chromosomes; some fungi, for

Travillion's Black Jack.

Grand Champion Mammy.

Behne's Clyde keeping a watch on things from the window.

example, have only a single set. On the other hand, other organisms have multiple sets, more than two. Such aberrations really were a problem for the pioneers in genetic research. Our cells, and those of the dog, have paired chromosomes, but our cells that transmit our traits, that is, our sex cells (and those of the dog) have only a single set. A cell with a single set of chromosomes is called a haploid cell; one with two sets is called diploid. Our general body cells, thus, are diploid, while our germ (sex) cells are haploid. When the body cells divide, the chromosomes duplicate themselves, remaining attached at a spot called the centromere. The membrane around the nucleus dissolves, and a fibrous spindle forms on which the chromosomes line up. The centromeres divide as the spindle fibers tug the chromosome pairs apart. The chromosomes arrive at the opposite poles and the spindle disperses. The nuclear membrane reforms, the chromosomes unwind within, and the cell divides, each containing the same original sets of chromosomes and each a duplicate of the other. This process is called mitosis.

Sperm and egg cells are single cells which are haploid (only half the normal number of chromosomes). They are known as gametes, as each carries a half set of chromosomes. At fertilization, their nuclei unite, giving the fertilized egg, or zygote, a full complement of chromosomes. From this single cell arise all the others by mitosis. There is a special kind of cell division just for making gametes. This process, called meiosis, is actually a double division. As in mitosis, the chromosomes double; but then the chromosomes pair off. Again the spindle fibers form, and the chromosome "tetrads" line up, and the pairs are *separated*. When they reach the poles, the spindle vanishes, and new spindles form the other way (along another plane). The chromosomes then separate, as in mitosis. Meiosis results in *four* cells, each with half the chromosomes of the original. Whichever copy ("homolog") of each chromosome goes to which cell is completely random. Any combination is as likely as the next. That is good for the process of evolution, for it provides the random variations from which the most adapted organisms will be favored. It is the basis for selective breeding, too. It is useful to know that there is going to be random variation on each side of the trait for which we are breeding.

Show Champion Dugan is also a weight pull ace.

Many simple traits are expressed by a single gene. However, we have pairs of genes just as we have pairs of chromosomes. Color is an example of a simple trait in dogs. The brindle color is always dominant over red. But we all know that brindle dogs bred to red ones don't produce all brindles. The reason for that is that the brindle dog may have had a genotype of **Bb**. That is, he had one gene for the brindle coloration and one for red. If he passed a red gene to a red female, a red pup will be the and some reds, with possible buckskins or whites, over which red is dominant. The genotype of the brindles could be either **BB** or **Bb**, but the genotype of the reds would be all **bb** (two genes recessive to brindle). It has to be that way, because if any of the pups had a brindle gene, it would "mask" the effects of the red gene, and the pup would be brindle.

Now this type of inheritance refers to simple traits only, and it is sometimes called simple Mendelian

"The Great One." Garrett's Champion Jeep, one of the greatest dogs of all time, pictured here at ten years old.

result. A brindle dog that has only brindle alleles ("traits") will produce all brindle dogs when bred to a red female. In the shorthand of genetics, the dog would be **BB**; he would be called homozygous because both genes are the same. The pups from such a mating would consist of all brindles, but their genotype would be **Bb**. (Genotype refers to the dog's genetic characteristics and phenotype refers to his observable traits, such as appearance and behavior.) The pups from such a mating if later bred together would produce some brindles (about 75% on the average) inheritance, in honor of Mendel, the Catholic monk who discovered the mechanism. However, the traits we are breeding for in Bulldogs all involve countless genes. So it is senseless to talk about whether gameness is recessive or dominant. It is polygenetic and, for that reason, it can't be characterized as either dominant or recessive. If it were a simple trait, either dominant or recessive, it would be quite easy to "lock it in" and all dogs would be game. The same applies to other traits such as hard bite or wrestling ability. They are complex traits involving many genes, and it is for that reason that breeding Bulldogs is a real challenge.

For this reason I think it is very important to use brood stock whose breeding can be verified, and that the ancestry of the stock is of top quality. It is not easy to find such animals, as too many people make compromises. There are few breeders who consistently produce a high percentage of deeply game dogs. Past breeders have done it utilizing a variety of breeding techniques, but all the successful

advancing your breeding program. In selective breeding, I envision working with a sieve every time we get an outstanding individual. We don't know what the companion genes are, but we know that the dog has the genetic material to be the great one that he is. For that reason, I would much prefer to breed to an ace that is the son of an ace than to his sire. The more great dogs we can get back to back in that manner (and among the females also), the better are our chances of getting good

A good kennel set-up owned by Tom Ludberg of Dallas, Texas.

ones were absolute cranks about the quality of their breeding stock.

One of the myths about breeding good animals is that rather than breed to an outstanding dog, you should go back to the dog that produced him. In my view, selective breeding is a matter of playing the percentages; there is no doubt that it is a percentage game; and geneticists become quite expert at statistical mathematics. But you are constantly striving for improvement of a line. If you go back to the dog that produced the ace, you are, in effect, standing still. You may get some good dogs, but you aren't

progeny. We have improved our percentages, because the average of the line is now better. A good rule of thumb is that you are generally going to get in the quality of your pups the average of the quality of the ancestry of the animals which are being bred. That is why aces are such disappointing sires. An ace is a once-in-a-life-time dog, but everyone expects him to sire "chips off the old block." Obviously, he is not going to do this unless he comes from an ancestry that includes all aces—and I know of no dog that has such a pedigree!

One thing that makes a dog a

Above: Dollie's Stained Glass, owned by Chris Harrod. *Opposite:* Red Dawson and a pure Panama Red bitch. (Panama Red was a noted pit dog.)

Jane and Carly Burke with Burke's Pepple.

prepotent sire, such as Dibo and Tombstone, is that the dog is homozygous in all the traits that make a good pit dog—or for at least most of the traits. As I've said before, there must be an enormous amount of genes which makes a good Bulldog, and those who talk about a "gameness gene" are completely ignorant of the mechanics of inheritance.

THE ACTUAL BREEDING

The best way to start breeding a game line of Bulldogs is to obtain the very best bred bitch (and, better yet, have her be of high quality, too, as she will become part of the pedigree of the pups) and breed to the top sire to which you have access. Your sire should be a candidate for the best dog in the country, both individually and from a breeding standpoint. For that reason, it is very unlikely that he will be found in your own kennels. Thus, your bitch will have to be taken to the stud dog. This can present problems with a good bitch. Most bitches, when in full heat, will stand for males with which they are familiar, but they will fight a Bulldog male who is a stranger to them. (Don't count on their fighting off all the cur dogs that may come around, though, as they will sometimes be more receptive to a cur, sensing somehow that he would be no competition anyway.)

So there is the problem of the actual breeding of the bitch. A muzzle should be handy. A man who owns a stud dog that is in demand will quite likely have a breeding box at his place. This simply consists of a rectangular box that you can place the bitch in, with her head sticking out through a hole in the end. It contains a locking mechanism to keep the bitch from getting around to the male. Even with this handy device, it can be nearly impossible to make the breeding, even with an experienced and cooperative male. It may be necessary to hold the bitch's hindquarters up by supporting her underneath the belly. Someone else may be needed to keep her hindquarters steady from each side. I have seen as many as six men trying to hold one little bitch, and it was difficult to say who was going to end up having the pups! The sacrifice of dignity is just one of many compromises that must be made in order to breed a good line of Bulldogs.

I like to keep the breeding natural if possible. It may be worth the risk to allow the animals to be together unrestrained. If you keep the bitch turned away from the male (in the former method), all the time restraining her, you can just about

Sam with his offspring—a father and son picture.

205

guarantee that she isn't going to be friendly to him. The natural way is worth a try (if the owner of the stud agrees to it), for it can make the breeding much easier on everybody concerned. The best way to use the natural method is to put the bitch in a kennel run. Then bring the stud dog up on leash to the run and let him approach naturally. He will be very interested in the smell she is disseminating, so he will sniff around and urinate a lot in areas the female can smell. This is "foreplay" with dogs, as they are very olfactory-oriented animals. Even a very aggressive bitch can usually be "seduced" by this approach. Once she starts acting friendly and receptive, the stud dog can be let in the kennel run off lead. Of course, you are taking a small chance that a fight will erupt, but that is easily terminated with two knowledgeable men and a pair of breaking sticks. Some breeders, in frustration and desperation, have taken to breeding by artificial insemination. That may be the easy way out, but I hate to see the American Pit Bull Terrier breed become so artificial that it must always be bred in that way.

THE BITCH IN WHELP

When a bitch is bred, one of the things that I first do is innoculate her against viral diseases, such as parvovirus, because that will enable her to pass on a limited immunity, at least, to the pups.

Another necessity is to take the bitch off the chain, whether on axle or cable, and place her in a kennel run. This is so the chain doesn't injure the pups. I have generally found a chain-and-cable set-up to be superior to any other method of keeping kennel dogs; however, a kennel run is absolutely essential for a bitch with pups.

Occasional bitches of all breeds will be unsuitable mothers. Most Bulldog bitches are good mothers, as good as any breed, but there is one hazard with the fight-crazy bitches, and it is that in the midst of a frenzy to get at another dog, they will grab up a pup and kill it. I have never had a bitch do this, but I have utilized only game bitches, and they seem more calm and keep their heads even when excited.

All bitches of all breeds occasionally lie on their pups and kill them. This usually happens with first-time mothers. The bitches that have had several litters normally become good at being careful with the pups. For that reason, I have abandoned the use of a whelping box for keeping the bitch with her pups. A whelping box is a large rectangular box with rails all around to keep the bitch from squeezing a pup against the sides. Personally, I feel the main success for the whelping box is that it is so large. So I do try to have an extra large doghouse, nearly the size of a whelping box, for the bitch in whelp. In my opinion (and certainly many people may disagree here), the rails are an unnecessary complication.

It is common belief among humans that other mammals don't suffer giving birth as do humans. It has been my observation that such is not necessarily true. Mammals have paid

Opposite: **A Bulldog generally makes a good parent. Owner, Brenda McLendon.**

Pogo, when he first arrived at his new home.

a heavy price for such exquisite protection of their young. Not only does a bitch suffer, but having too many litters can shorten her life. For that reason, I pick the breedings for my brood bitches very carefully and don't breed them often.

In any case, a bitch undergoing labor should be made as comfortable as possible. If you are emotionally close with your bitch, as you should be if you are any sort of dog man, you can stay with her during her labor, talking to her, comforting her, and just letting her know that she isn't going through this alone. A lot of Bulldog men will laugh at such advice, as will other dog people. Long experience has led me to my opinion, and I feel that even these Bulldog bitches, tough as they are, are entitled to every—and a little extra—consideration.

CARE OF THE PUPS

While the bitch is actually giving whelp is the time to give her the privacy she needs. She will work much better without your being under foot. It is the nature of all bitches to crave privacy with their babies after the exhaustive labor process.

A change will normally come over the bitch after she has her pups. She will still be glad to see you, but her instinct is to protect her babies, and she will be very nervous about your handling the pups. She may even place her body between you and the pups. It is easy to get hurt feelings about a bitch that you love and that you felt loved you acting as though she doesn't trust you, but it must be remembered that it is her instinct. We all know instincts are tough to deny. She knows you're okay, but something tells her to protect those babies anyway. One consolation is that I've never had a bitch go so far as to even growl, let alone bite. In deference to the bitch's feelings and instincts, I don't insist on handling the pups for several days.

I like to keep the pups nursing as long as possible—from the mother's milk they obtain immunity from ailments. Still, there is a natural age for weaning, and there will come a time that the mother is less and less inclined to nurse. When the bitch shows this inclination, I separate the pups from her, but I allow her in with them at night. In that way, she receives respite from the pups but still provides nourishment and the invaluable immunity.

Make sure your puppy pen is not under a tree or any other place where birds might nest, as droppings from these animals can carry a variety of diseases, primarily *coccidiosis.*

Your pups should receive their basic innoculations after they've been completely weaned from the bitch. In the meantime, you've supplemented the bitch's milk with warm milk mixed with a good grade of puppy food.

During their weaning period, wolves feed their young by regurgitating food. For that reason, the pups' licking at the bitch's mouth will sometimes cause her to regurgitate, but this rarely happens with Bulldogs, as they have been domesticated so long that this trait seems to be mainly lost.

Scientific investigation has revealed that it is important for puppies that are to be pets to receive their human socialization at the age of six to eight weeks. Pups that are to be sold for this purpose should be taken at this time. Remember, a responsible breeder will be very selective about to whom he sells Bulldog pups and will work closely with them afterwards, too. The failure to do this is part of the problem facing the breed today.

Christina and Hansel William with Koty.

Above: Swinney's Buster, a son of Sherwood's Popeye. Owner, Matt White. *Opposite:* Damien, a renowned pit dog to stud, is a son of Champion Crash and is down from Wallace's Bad Red on his mother's side.

A Good Boy Gone Bad

> *"The secret of happiness is this: let your interests be as wide as possible, and let your reactions to the things and persons that interest you be as far as possible friendly rather than hostile."*
> BERTRAND RUSSELL

Several years ago I started a series of stories on my experiences with dog men from the time that I first began with the dogs over forty years ago. The series was entitled "A Good Boy Gone Bad or How I Became an American Pit Bull Terrier Fancier." I didn't really mean that I had gone "bad." I have used similar titles on articles about some of my other interests, ones that have no taint of infamy to them. Bulldog people are long-suffering because of the unsavory nature attributed to them and because of a number of hysterias about the Bulldog that have run rampant, but they remain generally cheerful and endure the pain of the situation by joking about the absurdity of it all.

I had originally intended to reprint the series of articles, but they simply became too voluminous to reprint in a book of this type. For that reason, I will simply summarize some of what I told about the old-time dog men.

In Arizona, where my father was

STB's Rooster is a grandson of Grand Champion Hope and a son of Patrick's Rojo.

working as an immigration inspector, I originally became aware of the fact that there existed such a terrific breed. The head of the Border Patrol at that time kept gamecocks and a number of Bulldogs. However, I didn't acquire a dog of my own until we were living in Colorado.

My first dog was acquired from Louis Colby, with money I had obtained working a paper route while attending school.

In my almost fanatical interest in Bulldogs, I soon uncovered the fact that there was a magazine, *Bloodlines Journal*, which was put out by the United Kennel Club and contained substantial articles about the American Pit Bull Terrier breed. Through that publication, I discovered the book *Thirty-five Years with Fighting Dogs*, which George Armitage had had printed privately and was advertising in *Bloodlines*. I well remember the book arriving in the mail in its green cover, and my father commented that it wasn't much of a book for four dollars! In

those days it did seem like a small book for that much money. However, it was like gold to me, and I read and reread it voraciously.

I learned of William Lightner's existence in Colorado Springs, and I believe I wrote him a note and then traveled down by bus to see him.

The Lightners were delightful people, and they were both extremely interested in the dogs and had been long-time breeders of them. I didn't realize at the time just how good their dogs were or how esteemed were those people in the dog game. The Lightners eventually gave me a little female which I kept for several years.

Through Lightner, I met Winstead of Denver and Ed Weldon of Wyoming. Through Winstead, I met Pete Cain and other dog men in the Denver area. In those days, however, the dogs were not so popular nor so numerous, so dog men were pretty spread out. In those days, all people who kept Bulldogs were to a greater or lesser degree involved in pit contests. That is, if they didn't match dogs themselves, they obtained their dogs from those who did; and just the very fact that one kept a Bulldog was an indication of some degree of tacit approval of dogfighting. Yet there were no mean dogs and no incidents of attacks on people.

It has become an extremely widespread misconception that dogfighting created people-mean dogs; however, the fact that the dogs' natures were absolutely sound in an era in which all of them were of pit strains soundly refutes that idea.

During my boyhood years, I met a number of dog men, and I also developed a steady correspondence with many of them. One of these was Bert Clouse, who eventually visited Denver, and I traveled down to meet him and was included in the dog talk as though I were a grown man. Bert sent me pictures of his Big Boy and Kito dogs, and I eventually used them, some forty years later, in one of my books. But Bert was never one for breeding dogs, as he was more the kind who would refer to himself

Young's Southern Bad.

as an "action man." He liked the matches and didn't have time for raising pups.

When I entered the military in 1950, I sent my dog Spook down to I.D. Cole in Arizona, as I had been corresponding with him. When I left basic training and was on my way to Fort Campbell in Kentucky, I stopped off to see Cole for a couple of days; it was at that time that I met Howard Heinzl, S.W. Hubbard, and

Williams from the time he lived in Denver. He was one of the more responsible dog men in Colorado, but he was not part of the general group, as everyone else kept Lightner dogs. The fact that he kept a different line of dogs tended to separate him from the others. Besides, in retrospect, I can see that he was the seasoned old timer, whereas my friends were the youngsters of that day. However,

A Bulldog's natural tendency is to pull hard on a leash, and some owners don't mind that, as both dog and dog walker get more exercise that way.

Earl Prentice. Actually, there was an incredible number of dogs and dog men in Phoenix as compared to Colorado. In my opinion, it was no accident that the famous Dibo and White Rock, to mention just two famous dogs, came from that area. It is of interest that both those dogs came from Howard Heinzl.

My basic training had taken place in Fort Ord, California, and while there, I traveled down to visit with Jack Williams, a man who had dedicated himself to keeping the Con Feeley strain pure. Dogs from Williams were later to appear in the pedigree of Dibo. I had known Jack

Williams had been a special friend of mine and the source of information on many of the old-time stories and traditions about the breed.

Jack Williams was close friends with Howard M. Hadley, who became prominent as a Staffordshire Terrier fancier. However, his heart always remained with the old pit dogs; he was both a scholar and a great source for information on the dogs. Hadley was the nephew of H.L. McClintock of Oklahoma, generally considered one of the greatest breeders of all time and a real authority. I never met McClintock,

Rick Johnson with his Buddy dog.

but I saw many of his letters through Hadley. In addition, I was able to absorb some of McClintock's ideas from Hadley and from McClintock's very rare, but valuable, articles in *Bloodlines*.

It turned out that Howard Hadley was close friends with Bob Wallace of Little Rock, Arkansas, and he occasionally visited with him there. When I left California, I had a letter of introduction to Bob Wallace, one

Carroll's Breen is a dog in England.

of Hadley's closest friends in the breed, and a man whom Hadley considered a candidate for the greatest of the modern breeders.

I was understandably eager to make the trip down to Wallace's place; however, I met him first at a match in Tennessee. But later I made many visits to his beautiful home, and I became quite close to him and his wife. In fact, theirs became my home away from home, and they became nearly foster parents to me, as they were childless, and we got along quite well.

An interesting point is worth mentioning here. I often traveled with a friend with whom I had entered the military. He was not really a dog man, but his curiosity was aroused about the idea of fighting dogs. For that reason, he had made some of the visits to Louis Sylvestri's home in San Francisco, to Hadley's place in Covina, and Wallace's place in Little Rock. Sylvestri was a very successful businessman, and his home was absolutely palatial. Hadley's place was quite impressive, too, and Wallace's home, though basically modest in comparison, was a wonderful showcase for some fine dogs. My friend was curious as to why these dog men were all so "well heeled," I think was the way he put it. I smiled to myself when he asked about that, as it was mere circumstances that had allowed him only to see the more wealthy members of the fraternity. From my observation, the dog game is one that belongs to the working class.

It may have been hard to convince my friend of that, however, as he managed to meet me at some of the conventions that took place regularly at Leo Kinard's place. Kinard was known primarily as a gambler, but he also had real estate property and a drive-in restaurant (with the waiters on roller skates!). His home was situated beside a lake, and he kept 250 Bulldogs there. He had two full-time employees taking care of the dogs and the grounds. The pit that he had built for the conventions was quite plush for those days. This was before air-conditioning, but huge fans were built into the building's walls to help keep the inside cool; the housing of the fans was surrounded by wet straw, so that there was cooling by evaporation.

I attended many conventions during my time in the service, as it turned out that my company commander was a Bulldog

Takithat with her dog Ebony.

aficionado, too. During all this time, I met many dog men, some of whom were famous at the time, and others, such as Maurice Carver, who were to become famous in later years.

Although I was unable to keep dogs during the time I was in the military, it was, for me, a time of study and learning in regard to the dogs. I was able to meet so many people and attend so many conventions that were in easy reach of where I was stationed.

Later, when I was out of the military, I attended the University of Colorado, but even then, I couldn't keep my mind completely off the dogs and managed to keep one or two during the time that I attended school. One of them got me a personal meeting with Dr. George Gamov, a man of massive intellect. Once he made a comment to Albert Einstein that stopped him dead in his tracks in the middle of a busy street. Einstein had immediately seen the profound nature of the comment, and it so absorbed him that he forgot where he was! Gamov is an important figure in science today for several reasons. One of these is for his theories, since

verified, on nucleosynthesis, purported that new elements are formed in stars. Another idea that he popularized was that of the Big Bang as a theory of the beginning of the universe.

In my opinion, the man was nearly of the same rank as Einstein, but I was not a physics graduate student, so there was just no way I could attend a class of his. So how did the Bulldog arrange a meeting? Gamov had a son who had a German Shepherd which happened to jump my dog. My dog was on a chain, and the son (who was about my age) had his dog running loose. The German Shepherd was not really injured badly, but he was bloody and his owner was quite upset. When I visited later with the fellow, I was astonished to see Gamov there. But I was gratified that he rebuked his son gently, telling him that, after all, his dog had initiated hostilities, and it wasn't the first time for him to do that. Gamov reminded me of Joe Corvino in build, and I think he was amused that a little dog would have cleaned house on a big German Shepherd like the one that belonged to his son. Anyway, it allowed me to

Cracker won a national weight-pulling title.

Kona climbs a fence to see if the grass is greener on the other side.

spend some time talking to the great one, and I received sort of a private lesson on nucleosynthesis and quantum physics, as Gamov was delighted that I had read two of his books and treated me very well.

Later on in life, through my books, the dogs introduced me to many fascinating people, some of them famous, some of them not. But all of them have been deeply valued.

Kale Veronie with Agnes, a great-granddaughter of Plumber's Champion Alligator.

Gaddy's Buckshot Red is a dog of Old Family Red Nose breeding.

Above: Heinzl's Gypsy, by Heinzl's Bummy out of Tempe Tesse. *Opposite:* Maska's Sadie.

Worth Preserving

> *"Freedom of criticism cannot be denied without endangering the progress of human society."*
>
> CHAPMAN COHEN

The following are essays that appealed to me for various reasons, and I thought they would be of interest to the readers of this book. Articles that appear in magazines are usually evanescent, and it is my hope that some of these articles will be preserved for a longer period of time by appearing in a reference book of sorts on the American Pit Bull Terrier.

DEBATE . . .

This first is a debate initiated by a person who likes Bulldogs, but wanted to discuss the merits of some of the statements I made in former books. It was my thought that the points would be of interest to the reader. The debate continues at this time, so it is not as though I got in the last word. The writing originally appeared in the American Pit Bull Terrier Gazette.

McDonald states:

Open letter to Mr. Stratton: In *The World of the American Pit Bull Terrier* (T.F.H. Publications, Neptune City, NJ), Chapter 12, "The Face of Cruelty," Richard F. Stratton states on page 241, "Sometimes I feel ashamed of myself for the way I berate humaniacs, chasing them up hill and down dale, challenging them to debates that they furtively side step".

A maniac has an eager desire for something. I presume if that something is the humane treatment of all living things, one is a humaniac. I admit it, I am a humaniac and I will not side step a debate with anyone on the responsibility we, as supposedly intelligent human beings, have taken on ourselves in domesticating the canine and manipulating its genes for our purposes.

Pit-dog men argue that there is no cruelty involved in dogfighting because the dogs like to fight, want to fight, choose to fight. The philosophical question of man's free choice, as opposed to being a simple product of genetic and environmental conditioning, has been debated long and hard by those more learned than myself. The question of free choice for the pit bull is less complex. Man has selectively bred them to be highly aggressive to their own species and deficient in the gene for surrender and flight. Human intervention by genetic manipulation has brought about loss of choice for these animals. Environmental manipulation is constant. These dogs spend their entire lives chained, their movement severely restricted, in close proximity to other aggressive, equally frustrated animals. Their aggressive natures are constantly stimulated, then frustrated. The only activity possible for these animals is lunging at the end of their chains in frustration. Muscle and mental frustration result, both positive attributes in the fighting dog. Dogfighting aside, I question the kindness in providing a loving animal with this type of life-long existence.

Mr. Stratton goes on to say, on page 242 of the same chapter, that "No doubt the humaniacs feel that the pit-dog men are merely crying crocodile tears when their dogs are destroyed by animal welfare groups, but they really do *care* about their

Young's Geronimo.

Larry Bell with Winn's Red Neck.

dogs, not only as *individual* dogs for their own personality, but also because some of the destroyed dogs were famous among pit-dog men and were universally venerated." [italics inserted by McDonald.] The sincere loss felt is not in doubt, since not only are these dogs venerated for their fighting prowess but, they are also of great value, having had a lot of time and money invested in their acquisition and keep.

I hope "humaniac" means "having an eager desire for humane treatment" and does not mean illogical "madness." For illogical madness is the only way to describe the destruction of any living thing on the grounds that it is possessed by a cruel master. I agree with each and every word Mr. Stratton has written concerning the radical, publicity hungry, money hungry, humane organizations and their media vendetta against a breed. On what grounds are individual dogs killed

An athletic Bulldog demonstrating the great agility and determination that are characteristic of the breed.

Hammonds's Willie Son is sired by Hammonds's Willie Boy.

and an entire breed put in jeopardy for the cruel acts of their masters? The word "humaniac" can simply not be applied to these people as there is nothing humane about restrictive laws inhibiting man's constitutional freedom or the unjust destruction of animals. Madness yes, humane, no. Since becoming familiar with the plight of the American Pit Bull Terrier, I have given not one more penny to the Society for the Prevention of Cruelty to Animals or the Humane Society.

I will however contest Mr. Stratton's statement that the pit-dog men *care* about their dogs, particularly as individuals. Webster's Dictionary offers the following definition of the word *care*: implying concern for *safety*. *Safety* is defined as: exemption from injury. Having witnessed pit contests, would you, Mr. Stratton, consider retracting your statement that pit-dog men *care* about their dogs?

As far as the *individual* dog is concerned, I have heard pit-dog men argue that fighting their dogs to retain gameness, which makes them a distinctive breed and is supposedly correlated with the wonderful qualities of the breed, necessitates the sacrifice of *individual* dogs for the long term overall good of the breed. *The end justifies the means*—another age old philosophical argument rears its head! Mr. Stratton referred to it on page 109. Hitler believed that, and a good portion of civilized society disagreed with him.

Animals, domestic and otherwise, are exploited by humans for food, clothing, work, science, pleasure, and gain, and have been throughout history. But, in doing so, do we not, as supposedly superior, intelligent beings with supposedly god-given souls, have a moral and ethical responsibility to see that care is taken, either because of humanitarian concern or in order to abide by humane animal welfare acts, to prevent undue pain. I believe that to intentionally expose animals, for whom we are responsible, to physical injury for entertainment, gambling gains, and the preservation of gameness, having no scientific proof that gameness has any other purpose is *cruel*.

The definition of the word *cruel* is: disposed to give pain to others in body, causing pain. One has to assume that the injuries suffered by Pit Bulls in pit contests must give some pain. Since the pain is caused by exposure to the pit situation by pit-dog men, does that not mean that pit-dog men are cruel?

Again in chapter twelve, on page 245, Mr. Stratton says, "Perhaps there is cruelty . . . why is it that people who know absolutely nothing about it can see it so clearly?"

Perhaps I should clarify why I feel I don't fit the category of those who know nothing about it. I live with Pit Bulls. I have met at least fifteen pit-dog men and have been privileged to visit their yards. I have studied Pit Bull pedigrees, marvelling at the genetic science applied in the development of the breed and have sat in on many a discussion about breeding, gameness, keeps, rolls and matches; I have seen the equipment used for conditioning and admired good keeps. I have been instructed in the proper use of the breaking stick and helped break up yard fights. I read the *Pit Bull Gazette*, other pit dog magazines, and Mr. Stratton's books and articles. I know and love many individual Pit Bulls and recognize the many wonderful qualities inherent in the breed, although I don't necessarily believe that they can be correlated to

Misty is of Neblett-Creed-Colby bloodlines.

gameness. I fear:

1. The stupid felony laws which make dogfighting more of a crime than those perpetrated against man, and fear, even more

2. Discriminatory, restrictive legislation against one breed of dog because of the activities of those who choose to own them. But I do think that pit-dog men are *cruel*.

that were making the ridiculous statements about Bulldogs being mean, their "trainers" utilizing electric prods to make them fight, and kittens, together with pigeon blood, to bring out their "blood lust"! Another favorite description was that, on the way to the pit, pit-dog men kicked their dogs repeatedly, because "mean dogs win;

Bellisle's Buddy.

If Mr. Stratton is willing to respond to my rambling and your readers find it of any interest to read the humaniac's side, I am willing and able, having herein looked only at one chapter of his three books, to further dissect the writings of Mr. Stratton, which I understand represent the generally held beliefs of the pit bull fraternity.—Grace L. McDonald, Redsky Kennels Reg's Exclusively Yellow Labrador Retrievers, Canada.

Stratton replies:

When I was ranting and raving, trying to get humaniacs to debate me about some of the outrageous things they were saying, I meant the dumb ones! After all, they were the ones

nice dogs don't"! (Anyone who makes a statement like that doesn't only not know anything about Bulldogs, but he is woefully ignorant in his knowledge of dogs generally.) Anyway, it was people of this ilk who I wanted to debate, and I preferred that it take place in *their* magazines, where their own readers could get a chance to hear the other side (and, perhaps, see what frauds their writers were). But, what do I get? I get a smart humaniac who is obviously educated and knows all about the implication of such philosophical concepts as free will and determinism and whether or not "the end justifying the means" is a tenable position. Still, I guess I've stuck my head in the noose, so I must make some attempt, however feeble,

Bud, owned by Phil Chaves.

James Kelly with a granddaughter of the great Alvin dog.

Right: A typical
Heinzl dog.
Below: Carlene
Freeman and
Black Beauty.

At a San Jose dog show, we find an example of the more common small Pit Bull.

to extricate myself. One of the things that makes this exchange a little unfair is that Mrs. McDonald is not really a humaniac at all. Since I coined the word, I guess I can define it, and by it I meant those people who were absolutely maniacal in their defense of what they perceived as humaneness. They were thus willing to euthanize Bulldogs "for their good," and they were absolutely eager to put pit-dog men in prison and throw away the key! Mrs. McDonald has disavowed all

that, so she is not (alas!) a humaniac. She is just concerned about the mistreatment of animals, as I am also—believe it or not!

Regarding the free choice issue, it so happens that I am one of those who regards "free will"—even in humans—as an illusion, and I think most research psychologists and psychiatrists would agree with me; however, it is not an important point. But I do think that it takes a certain amount of convoluted reasoning to say that we have taken free choice

Champion Gnasher is a three-time winner in England.

away from the dogs by breeding them to enjoy fighting. I mean, did Mrs. McDonald's retrievers "choose" to enjoy fetching so much and to have such an unusual interest in birds? (And remember, Bulldogs have been bred for this for at least hundreds, and probably thousands, of years. So the breed existed pretty much as it is now when we were born, when our parents were born, when our grandparents were born and etc.) I think saying that Bulldogs were bred deficient in the gene for

flight or surrender is misreading the evidence. But let us digress for a moment. The animals with the best developed flight response are those such as mice and minnows. The poor things flee at every movement and are terrified of every shadow. Other animals, such as the tiger, elephant, and killer whale, however, have almost no flight response, mainly because they don't really need it. But even these animals will run away from something such as fire, so they are not completely without fear.

Bulldogs, too, incidentally, will get away from such obvious hazards, and they show normal fears of things such as height. Of course, most of them have more grit than most breeds about nearly any activity, but the point is they are not without a self-preservation instinct, contrary to what many writers have declared. One thing that may cloud the issue here is that there are dogs that will do such things as attack a power mower or a locomotive! What is going on here, in my opinion, is that the old hunting instinct is making itself felt. After all, these dogs were used for wild boar and animals; hence, a certain percentage of them are ready to tackle anything rambunctious that isn't human. Anyway, it is simply human nature to exult in the "tiger burning bright" and to pity the mice. The Bulldog, then, is a tiger, and there are few people who don't admire his courage. It has taken countless years, many human generations in fact, to develop, so it certainly was not simply a matter of elimination of a single gene. To the contrary, the Bulldog, I am certain, has been built by breeding into him complex mechanisms that allow him to have such incredible stamina and strength and to be able to override pain in the heat of battle.

Mrs. McDonald speaks of how she has seen Bulldogs kept and she disagrees with what she has seen. I can only assure her that there is as much variety in how Bulldog people keep their dogs as in any breed. I have seen kennel runs so big that the dogs didn't even wear down the grass. And of course, I've said many times that I thought Bob Wallace's cable-and-chain method was perhaps the best method of all for keeping any kennel dogs. I've also said that one of the cruelest aspects of keeping pit dogs is that most

people raise up a lot of them in order to be competitive and thus, they end up with a lot of kennel dogs that don't get a lot of attention. But that is also true of show people and sled-dog people, not to mention retriever people. However, I must admit that I don't have the negative attitude toward chains that Mrs. McDonald does. Even though I have kennel runs, I prefer a good chain setup, because the dogs get more touching and attention. They also usually have more square foot room.

I disagree that the dogs are constantly stimulated, then frustrated, in their desire to fight by being chained next to each other. The dogs get used to each other, and they don't pay much attention to one another; in fact, they can even become friends with the dog next to them. That is why when a dog gets loose, he often goes to a dog clear down to the other line of the chain, much to the astonishment of an owner who doesn't understand what's going on. Of course, some dogs are more aggressive than others, and don't really make friends with any other dogs; however, they do get used to their neighbors and only rail at them when they are excited. With such dogs, it doesn't take much to get them excited, and they can spend a lot of their time in *seeming* frustration, trying to get at the next dog. After many years of observing such things, I have dubbed this state as a sort of "delicious delirium." They seem to enjoy it. I have a little bitch that waits all day long so she can act like an idiot when I turn some of my other dogs loose, and she may be a trifle frustrated, but she certainly seems to enjoy fighting her dish, hitting the end of the chain, and just generally acting crazy. And that's her daily workout, after which she seems quite content. And I don't for one minute think that she is more

Right: Dagos Honey Suckle Rose being shown in a California ADBA-sanctioned conformation show. *Below:* Peltier's Show Champion Pooper with her conformation show winnings.

game than my other bitches.

As for my statement that most pit-dog men really care about their dogs, I meant that they have a love for them and do care about their welfare. It's true that they do match them in a contest that endangers their lives, but everything is relative. Some humaniacs would rail at Mrs. McDonald for allowing her dogs to swim (vicious currents and all that!). Good dog men match their dogs, care for them afterwards, and if the worst should happen, they mourn for them. (I've seen many a "hardened" pit-dog man administering to his dog with tears streaming down his face when he was worried about losing him.)

And I should mention that some pit-dog men have been fortunate enough to match dogs for years without losing one. It is not intended to be a fight to the death. The deaths that do occur are accidental and usually due to hypovolemic shock.

Finally, I must admit that some pit-dog men are more interested in hewing their own reputations than they are in the dogs, and some of them are insensitive jerks. Still, I can assure Mrs. McDonald that there are pit-dog men out there with far more compassion and far more responsibility than your average pet owner. And my experience certainly has been that gameness is directly

Buddy at 54 pounds.

Shreve's Cycle, a son of Captain Dick and Lucky Madam Red. Owner, Stephanie Shreve.

correlated with a rock-steady disposition and all the other traits that endear the Bulldog to us all— yes, even to the pit-dog men! Without gameness, Bulldogs become just another dog. And that brings us to the end's justifying the means. Personally, I don't think the argument is an absolute. I don't think any goal justifies any means necessary to achieve it. However, in this case, we are talking about allowing dogs to do something they like to do (albeit there may be a modicum of discomfort afterwards) and thereby revealing to their owners which is the best of them and thus, which ones to breed.

In the case of Mrs. McDonald's retrievers, an animal such as a pigeon or pheasant is shackled and thrown in the air to train the dogs. The dogs may like all this, but the pigeons and pheasants don't—at least, I would assume they do not. And certainly the ducks must not appreciate being shot down, as many are crippled and never found, even by a retriever, and are left to die a slow death—and *they* weren't bred to like any part of this. At least, with pit dogs, we have *only willing participants*, even if it was countless generations of breeding that made them the heroic and all-around wonderful creatures they are.

Left: Heinzl's Bull Dozer, a three-time pit winner. *Below:* A Pit Bull Terrier being shown at a recent dog show.

Roccas's Cherry Brandy, a game daughter of Ozzie Stevens's Solo and Rocca's Cherry Bomb.

Above: **Fouse's Rambo won a first place in a Louisiana weight pull.**

Below: **Rickie Contreras and his girlfriend with Trouble.**

A REASONED APPROACH TO CONDITIONING

Part One

This next is an article on conditioning that originally appeared in Sporting Dog Journal. *Many of the ideas contained herein were quite profound and new, too, to the pit-dog game. I had to prevail upon my friend Fred Maffie to be allowed to reprint the article, as he is now a successful freelance writer and author of books. He once matched pit dogs, so he speaks from experience. There is a lot to learn from Fred, both from this article and from his books.*

Maffie writes:

How does a dog man choose his conditioning program?

I don't know, let's ask him.

He'll tell you:

(a) It's the method that works best for him (practical, but one man's best is another man's ho-hum);

(b) It's the most used, most widely recognized method (traditional, everybody reminisce); or

(c) So-and-so does it that way (worshipful, everybody genuflect at mention of So-and-so's name).

That pretty much covers the spectrum, and it would seem, as they say, that truly there is nothing new under the sun, especially where it comes to conditioning a dog.

Even so, the conditioning of a match dog, if nothing new under the sun, is certainly something unique unto itself. Not even the fighting dog's human counterpart, the prizefighter, conditions in the exact same way, or even in a way that is very similar.

Imagine a dog wearing little mittens, rearing up and pawing a speedbag to blurring, or for that matter, a prizefighter tucking his wrists and straining his neck to work a hide!

You see how ridiculous it is. It's no good trying to compare the two, the two-legged prizefighter looking so spritely in his bright trunks, his four-footed counterpart in the altogether. There simply is no comparison. To call them the same is to rob the one of his most prized possession—his bright flash of trunks—to leave him standing there mortified to death, shoulders hunched, knees together, cupping himself; or else we fancy up an equally mortified Fido in a little twin suit of the same stripe and color, only of course we cut out a little hole for his tail. You see how wrong it all is. Why, the very thing that the one is most proud of, the other is most ashamed of! They are different, quite different, the match dog and the prizefighter. In the face of reason we concede the fact immediately.

Absolutely unique, the conditioning of the match dog—let no one deny it. And yet, conditioningwise, it seems to me that dog men are fairly bogged down in the ABCs of it—reminiscing, worshiping, and being practical ("practical" often meaning choosing the lesser of two evils). Nowhere, not ever, have I heard anyone outline for me a plan of conditioning designed specifically for the match dog, some reasoned approach that truly addresses all that is uniquely inherent to the matching of dogs and to bringing the match dog to his full potential.

Always it's something borrowed, tacked on—what our forebears did or what our modern-day heros do— or, for something more up-to-date in the scientific mode, what a swimmer, weightlifter, or track star does. And I suppose we're fairly satisfied with things as they are because . . . because . . . well, I guess for the simple reason that there truly is nothing new under the sun.

So there you have it, the long and the short of it—there is nothing new under the sun.

Poor old sun! Fat lot of good it does him being the bright fellow he appears, doomed to rise up again and again every twenty-four hours throughout all eternity and never to shine down upon anything new. A wonder the brightly bedecked little gentleman doesn't go cynical, so

Weight pulling has been a competition in which Pit Bulls, with their great strength and intensity, have excelled, often beating out dogs bred for the purpose.

Frank Rocca with Rocca's Dice.

much glum sameness in the world. How does he keep his happy face anyway, in the face of such gloom? Is he a mere idiot after all, a grinning idiot, gone senile after all these millenia of watching such culminating marvels of nature as you and I, dear reader, evolve?

Or wait just a mintue. On the other hand, his just might be a never-ending, life-giving, alive-as-the-moment wisdom that says: "Nothing new under the sun? What bosh! How about each new day—for starters!"

Somehow I like him much better that way, don't you? It feels right viewing him that way, I mean now that we're psychoanalyzing him.

By now you're probably impatient to tell me (as my wife just now has, having read what I've written so far) to stick to the point. Well, I promise that for the remainder of this article I shall keep my feet planted firmly and not go flying off to become the tail of some constellation, however great the temptation might be. Thank you, Hon, for bringing me back to earth . . . only the sun looked so jolly close up that I warmed to him

immediately and thought I'd stay and chat for a while.

All right.

Imagine for a moment that we are about to condition a dog. Only it's never been done before! We don't know the first thing about it. What would we do then, with no one to quote?—no one to emulate?

Interesting premise—being the first ever to condition a dog for matching. Farfetched? Not at all. We have only to realize that just because someone before us has held forth on conditioning, the mere fact of his having held forth doesn't necessarily make his findings correct. Realize that and—*voila!*—we are back at square one!

And that's just the sort of hard-nosed skeptics and die-hard solipsists we want to be. We want to know first of all *why* we do as we do—and then *to what effect*. We are going to question; we are not going to accept even the most basic premise, not till we've put it to the test anew. And then, if we have enough confidence in ourselves to have got this far without floundering, without feeling in desperate need of having a life preserver flung our way, we are going to believe fully in our intelligence, originality, ingenuity, and empathy with our dog to see us through.

(I might have mentioned empathy first, for without it we are not worth our salt as dog men. What are they saying to us, those eager brown eyes, as they look up so trustingly at us?

Remember, decent man or miserable lump of a man, in those trusting brown eyes we are each of us a god. We, at the outset, had better know the weight of our responsibility.)

And now that we have our scenario, I'll leave you to your own efforts. I cannot know what you would do if you were the first ever to condition a dog, but I do know what I would do, and in fact have done.

Banjo, a two-time winner who defeated Grand Champion Henry, running the treadmill. Owner, Jeff Fontenot.

Above: Lavasseur's Smokey, a U.K.C.-registered American Pit Bull Terrier.

Left: Hale's Oklahoma.

Above right: Adam's Billie Jean. *Right:* King Limeys Champion Smuggler, a three-time winner in England.

Before ever having matched a dog—before ever deciding that I actually would—I did over three years of extensive trial-and-error experimenting at how best to condition the match dog. And in that time I came up with what seemed to me a perfectly viable marriage of reasoning and realization, my own personal conditioning program, a method which I was able to refine more and more over the years that

efficacy, I believe wholeheartedly that my program shapes a dog as well or better than most methods you're likely to run into, and in comparison is safer, easier, and a whole lot more enjoyable for both man and dog.

Perhaps the best way to make my conditioning program readily understandable is to show first of all how it departs from the conventional.

Carl Griffirhi's Buck, sired by Skipper out of Beauty, is a 76-pound dog, an unusually large size for the breed.

followed, those years in which I was active in matching dogs.

Naturally, I kept my conditioning program almost exclusively to myself—and if I freely give it out now, it is because I no longer have you, dear reader, to worry about. I am now law abiding. Not because I'm being a good little boy, you understand. I simply have nothing more there to prove, and therefore no longer the inclination.

I don't know that my way qualified as something new under the sun, but it is certainly far removed from the more conventional methods. As to its

The usual way is to work your dog five or six days a week (sometimes twice a day), resting him one or two days. With my way, the exact reverse is true—I work my dog two days a week and rest him at least two or three days in between.

Immediately there is a vast difference between the two. So great a difference, perhaps, that some of you are already decided that balmy breezes play lightly in that space where my good sense ought to reside. Well, I won't deny it for a minute. Better a flight of fancy, I always say, than some hoary old idea weighted

Champion Zipper is a son of Grand Champion Zebo.

down by its very tonnage. To those of you so bolted down as to have already chosen up sides, I nod curiously, give a quick little wink, and cut another caper on the wind.

How much work and how often is best for our dogs? This is the heart of the matter.

In order to answer properly we need to examine what it is we expect of our dog. That's easy. We expect him to be able to fight for two or even three hours straight. We are working our dog so that one day he will be capable of three hours of strenuously dishing and taking it.

Austin's Junior.

Let me stress that we have our sights pinpointed on *one day*—one particular moment in time, thirty days from now—and it is a one-time shot!

We must begin the conditioning. Any sort of sparring being out of the question, we must settle upon some sort of *equivalent* activity in order to prepare our dog. So let us arbitrarily declare 25 to 30 miles of roadwork (to use the most common form of exercise) run in 2½ to 3 hours to be the equivalent of a dogfight. When our dog can do this we will consider him conditioned and capable of riding out a long hard match.

Again, the goal for us and our fight-ready dog is 25-30 miles in 2½-3 hours.

How do we reach our goal using the conventional method of working our dog every day? Well, the charts I've seen drawn up add just a bit more work every day, so many more miles, or, if mill work, so many more minutes. Presumably, and in the most simple terms, we might add one mile's distance to our dog's roadwork every day and so achieve our goal of thirty miles at the end of a thirty-day keep.

Now let me point out what I consider to be the drawbacks to this method:

We've already said that a dogfight is a one-time shot, takes place at one particular moment in time and then is finished. Yet it seems to me that the conventional method of daily work is more in keeping with working a dog toward some sort of *repeat* performance—sled pulling, for example—in which a dog is required to repeat the same grueling course day after day, perhaps three days in a row. If I were conditioning a dog to pull a sled, the conventional method of conditioning is the exact one I would choose. But seeing as how our dog is not to pull a sled, but rather to fight—and to fight for only one particular moment in time—and seeing as how we have already declared 30 miles in three hours to be the dogfight equivalent—it is our job to reach that goal as simply and painlessly as possible.

The conventional method does not do this. It is grueling repetition—and always there is the danger of overworking our dog. Day after day

Arsuffis Yipper winning a dog show class at 28 pounds.

Nell's ROM is a one-time loser but is valued for her gameness.

Right: This dog, placing at a conformation show, is the average sized Pit Bull. *Below:* Tucker, placing in his class at a conformation show to the delight of his young handler.

our dog is pushed and expected to gain just enough strength and endurance so that he can better, however slightly, his performance of the previous day. Till toward the end of the conditioning period we would have our dog repeating *daily* (if possible) the physical equivalent of a feat he is expected to perform but *once.*

Most times, and not surprisingly, we find that it is *not* possible for our dog to live up to these high expectations of ours. Nevertheless, we are insistent. We'll get around these ridiculous canine limitations somehow or other. It's no wonder, then, the workouts would be so *obviously* too much, and so a second workout later in the evening is required.

This too seems to me risky at best, the constant daily pushing a dog and then working him twice a day so that he might keep that precarious balance. For what it boils down to is that we have placed him at the very edge of his own physical limitations—and there he balances!

Further, splitting the workouts into twice daily is neither quantitatively nor qualitatively comparable to the actual workings of a dogfight. After all, there is no intermission in a dogfight. Except for the handles, the match continues. For this reason, I believe the workouts during the conditioning period ought to be self-contained and complete. Again, if your dog is matched in the morning and runs out of steam, you can't call time, rest him, and then come back that evening to finish the match. A workout—*one* workout—ought to simulate a dogfight as closely as possible.

Now let me quickly outline for you the method I prefer. I work my dog twice a week, increasing the amount of roadwork on those days roughly as follows:

1st day, 5 miles, *2nd day,* 5 miles, *3rd day,* 10 miles, *4th day,* 15 miles, *5th day,* 20 miles,*6th day,* 20 miles, *7th day,* 25 miles, *8th day,* 25 or 30 miles.

If I could think of any drawbacks to this method, I would have

Frances Travillion with her Jeb Stuart dog.

Frontenac's Gator Baby with owner Karen Block.

eliminated them long ago. So instead I'll list the advantages as I see them:

The principal factor making it possible for a dog worked in this manner to progress so easily to our goal of running 30 miles in under three hours is, in a word, *rest*—the generous amount of rest allowed between workouts.

There is a great difference, both in performance level and level of enthusiasm, in a dog that is worked every day and one that has been refreshed through two or three days' rest in between. If a dog has to really push in order to make five miles on one day, he is going to have hell making six the next, seven the next, etc. But let that same dog struggle through his five-mile workout, and then *rest him two days*, and on the third day he will jump for joy at sight of the harness and give you ten miles in joyous celebration!

Note that while the rested dog has, at this point, ten miles roadwork capability under his belt, the schedule of the dog being worked daily has in the same amount of time only brought him to a capability of eight miles. Here's how it compares:

Rested dog: *1st day*, 5 miles; *2nd day*, Rest; *3rd day*, Rest; *4th day*, 10 miles.

Other dog: *1st day*, 5 miles; *2nd day*, 6 miles; *3rd day*, 7 miles; *4th day*, 8 miles.

This discrepancy between the two is compounded steadily as the conditioning wears on.

And so it continues for the fully rested dog, the same added strength and lively enthusiasm through each session, each session progressing (roughly) in five-mile increments, and right on through to the final workout of 25 or 30 miles. This is the easiest, least painful, and safest way I can conceive of to bring a dog to the desired level of conditioning.

A final comparison of the two methods:

My way of thoroughly resting a dog brings him to the desired goal of 30 miles in three hours. So does the conventional method—*maybe*! However, my way reaches that goal in eight workouts (or less if we prefer, but it's best if the dog doesn't peak too early), my dog's roadwork amounting to roughly 110 miles total.

By the conventional method, assuming we start our dog at one mile the first day and add a mile each day until the goal is reached, we end up with 30 workouts and a total of 480 miles roadwork. (Of course these are arbitrary figures, my intention being to give a fair representation of the *rationale* behind the conventional conditioning program.)

Eight workouts and 110 miles total or 30 workouts and 480 miles total—assuming either way achieves the desired effect, which would you prefer?

I've already called this an article

Colby's Galtie II, bred and owned by Louis B. Colby.

Bruiser Smith ready for a pig hunt in Australia.

in two parts, and now, as I near the close of this quite lengthy part one, let me leave you with some food for thought.

On the question of how much work is too much or too little, let me point out that any well-kept, healthy dog ought to be able to go half an hour off the chain—and knowledgeable dog men of the past have fully conditioned their dogs with *just a bit of walking*, and with good results. Such men were well aware of the natural strengths of the bulldog even

when unconditioned, and they were also aware of the dangers of overworking the pit dog. Many of us have seen what can happen— "conditioned" dogs that would have done better off the chain!

On the other hand, it's certainly true that a dog can be put into fine shape by working him hard nearly every day. It's been done time and time again by good conditioners who know their dogs inside and out.

In short, there are any number of ways to shape a dog to pit readiness,

Hammonds's Brutus. Owner, Gary J. Hammonds.

and I don't dispute this. But what I'm saying is this: here is a way I consider to be safer and easier than any other conditioning program I know of, and it just might be well worth your considering it.

Again, as to the efficacy of my program, I'll state briefly that I used it my first time out, traveled 600 miles and stopped the Fowlers' bitch in an hour-forty-something-or-other. My bitch was solid on her feet and could have fought for another hour. My second and third times out, I conditioned two simultaneously and fought them on the same day, one right after the other—two wins.

I've heard others say how difficult it is to condition two dogs at the same time. Well, using my "resting method," I could have conditioned three or even four dogs simultaneously. I did not find it particularly difficult conditioning two dogs.

I did not win *all* my matches (a two-thirds win average), but I can truthfully say that I never lost one because I was outconditioned.

(You must bear with me for seeming to toot my own horn, but if I'm to quote known results of my method's having been applied, I have only my own personal experiences to relate.)

I've given you the basics of what seems to me a reasoned approach to conditioning, and submitted them for your review. I've made my presentation as simple and understandable as I could, even at times reducing the conditioning process down to an equation. All well and good. In some circles the equation is held in high regard, reverence even. It has its place, certainly. But let us not become idolaters. Personally, I've never used a chart, certainly never followed one religiously. I haven't met the equation yet that could tell me one mini-fraction of what the look in a dog's eyes has told me, and no equation ever grew a blister on its feet!

In other words, now that we've got the bare equation out of the way, it's time for us to elaborate on those aspects of conditioning that by far transcend the purview of mere chartdom

Jack Kelly, editor of *Sporting Dog Journal*, with his Champion Drummer.

Part Two

The contracts are signed. The forfeits are up. Now go to it! "C'mon, Dusty, you pretty little thing you! The fun begins!" The fun, the work, the closeness, that excited sense of determination that builds and builds—the conditioning! "Ready, ol' girl?"

I needn't ask. One look at her and I know. The wide bright eyes, the chain sharply alive, Dusty twisting, leaping over it jump-rope fashion! Oh, if just one time in my life I could express my joy as freely, as unreservedly as Dusty!

It's out on the road she's wanting, going down the open road ahead of the two-legger slowpoke dragging behind her. At this moment it's all she wants in all the world, it's all her passion. Dusty all eagerness wagging at the end of her chain, wagging to beat the band, one wild self-flagellating little bundle of pure joy. Then her burst of barking rallying me toward her, her sharp barks quickening, overbrimming, the nearer I get.

And if at that most crucial moment I should pause, seem to give my attention elsewhere, immediately

Stevens's Black Pearl, sister to Matlock's Truck.

Click's Josh.

she goes still and silent. Something in her eager little body just wilts. She looks longingly at me, hoping against hope that I haven't changed my mind, rendered the ultimate disappointment—canceled Christmas! That's the look she levels at me, fixes me with. And she stands stock-still, watching me, all her soul in abeyance.

A cruel bit of mischief leaving ol' Dusty hanging like that, but if we're to get into all this "how-to" stuff all over again we need to have a real dog waiting in the wings for us, reminding us, chiding us against wordiness, too much dawdling.

Patience, Dusty, we haven't forgotten you.

Anyway, it's roadwork we'll be using, not a treadmill. Why not a mill? Well, first of all, I don't own one. Never have. But that's not the main reason. If I had wanted a mill, I'd *have* a mill.

Someone offered to lend me one once when I was working the Tater bitch Tuffy—and I did use it to good advantage.

The first time I put Tuffy on the mill, she loved it—went all out! I took her off after 20 seconds! If I had worked Tuffy solely on the mill, I could have worked her *hard*. I would have had to watch her closely, contrived to settle her down some. I imagine she'd have settled into it properly in time—in the pit she was the best "pacer" I've ever seen, bar none. *But she did love that mill!* If I had allowed it, she'd have run herself into the ground time and again.

Which raises the question: at what point does building up become tearing down? Do you know the answer? Don't speak too quickly now; don't quote—think! I submit to you that it is difficult enough for you to know when you *yourself* in your *own* exercise program are under or overworking yourself—and you are the one actually *experiencing* the one or the other! The line between the two is a fine one upon which not even our best athletes can balance perfectly. But you would presume to know and recognize it in the case of your dog?!

I do not know precisely at what point building up becomes tearing down. I don't know and neither do you, for this is something we cannot know with total accuracy. This, however, I do know. If you believe in working your dog to near exhaustion, you've passed that fine line light years ago and thrown good sense out the window as well!

The mill stood idle through most of Tuffy's conditioning. Tuffy was, at best, a fair worker out there on the road trotting alongside my bicycle. Seldom was she ahead of me and she needed a glimpse of cat or squirrel in order for me to get a wind sprint out of her—at which time this flying Bronco Billy had to watch his *own* damn neck! So I'd trot Tuffy back to the house every now and again, put

Little Holly, a famous pit bitch.

Champion Pretty Boy Floyd (Champion Jack Hammer ex Mean Joleen).

Freeman's Rusty Red Boy without his sunglasses.

her on the mill for 2- or 3-minute wind sprints interspersed 2 or 3 times within a workout. It worked out quite well.

But generally I'm against mill work for the following reasons:

First, if you have a Tuffy-type, there is the obvious danger of overworking your dog. When your dog is overly excited and going all out, how better to exercise your own good sense of judgment than to remove the dog from the mill immediately! You know the heart and the spirit of these dogs. A good dog might push until he's on the verge of bursting heart and lung— and yet to watch his smoke you'd think he was on top of the world! Can you honestly say you can judge this situation to a safe degree of accuracy? I can't. Lend me your gauge! So with the mill there is a certain loss of control, a sense of something being out of hand.

Second, if our workout is to

simulate as closely as possible a dogfight, it means leaving our dog three hours on the mill (unless we use another type of work as well, fitting the mill work in as we choose). Three straight hours on a mill is too long a time for any dog.

Third, it seems to me the mill detracts from the personal relationship established between man and dog, that closeness that can be so important in the long haul. The mill is, after all, just a mechanical device. The more mechanical the method of conditioning, the less personal it is going to be. Where before you had a sense of connectedness with your dog, a true sense of touch and feel—the taut end of a leash in your hand—with the mill you have lost this. You cannot consistently *feel* the strength of your dog, or compare his strength of today with what it was last time out. The feel of the leash in the hand, this subtle communication, the impressions we receive, noted half subliminally perhaps, feelings that

struggle up, boding ill or good, vague discomforts with what we are doing, assurances that bring confidence— all this is ruled out with use of the mill. One of our precious senses, one whole irreplaceable field of personal input—our sense of touch— is denied us!

We were saying how the mechanical detracts from the personal. Indeed, the longer a dog stays on the mill, the more of an automaton he becomes. Did you ever see a dog left too long on a mill? His eyes appear almost sightless, mesmerized. Lift him off the mill and his legs keep moving! So some of us dog men are entering the field of robotics, are we? "I say there, pass the oil can, will you? My dog has developed a squeak!" Bah!

Finally, and this is a personal prejudice—I feel like a perfect numbnut standing about and letting all the activity belong to my dog alone. We are partners in this effort, are we not? I feel that any man who is able but unwilling to put a bit of

Toro, a one-time winner and a son of Malo's Clumpsy.

Above: Hammonds's Knockit, by Hammonds's Vito, a two-time winner, ex Hammonds's Chelsey. *Below:* Karyn Ketner and Riptide Stormy Boots, a granddaughter of Champion Little Boots. *Opposite:* Double D's Dorsey, by Holiday's Desperado ex Ford's Dancetown Dolly.

Locke's Miss Rooster.

muscle into it himself is in the wrong game after all. He ought to try something else, something more his speed. Raising gerbils, perhaps.

Actually, I could have elaborated a good deal more on what I consider to be the shortcomings of the treadmill. . . . But then we'd be forgetting good little Dusty waiting so patiently in the wings.

"Okay, Dusty! At long last!"

I wonder do the dogs ever wonder over that curious little dance step we dog men have become so adept at over the years—that life-saving, last-moment little sidestep we perform in order that some ecstatic little whirlwind like Dusty doesn't hit us with her forepaws right where it hurts the most.

That's the first and foremost instruction I would give to a beginner—and I give it even before we begin our outing—always protect the family jewels!

This is to be Dusty's final workout before matching. We've brought her along in accordance with the method described in Part One . . . I'm not going to spend time mentioning rudimentary "how-to" items such as pad tougheners, etc. In other words, if you can get it from a hundred other sources, I'd rather not waste your time and mine with a lot of boring repetition.

Away we go, Dusty, and this time we have some folks invited along. Dusty is a good worker, the best. She makes my part of it a snap. She doesn't start out too fast or too slow. She realizes we're going to be out a good while and paces herself accordingly.

Would that they were all so easy to work!

Too slow at the beginning is not so bad. It's warm-up time anyway and we want those muscles stretched, the kinks worked out before we really go at it. Too *fast* is no good at all. Consider. What is the *dogfight* equivalent of a dog's going all out at the beginning of his workout and then moping through the rest of it? The equivalent, fightwise, might well be the barnstorming loony that spends himself in twenty minutes, quickly changing his tune from "The Wrath of God is Upon You!" to "Oh Bail Me Out Daddy Please 'Cause My Mother's Done Conked Out and the Wrecking Crew is Here!"

Obviously the barnstorming loony is not a match dog and we ought not be conditioning him anyway. Even so, I can't stress strongly enough the importance of settling down even a good little dog that is perhaps too eager a worker. We don't want him exhausted before he's had a chance at his second wind. He must be made to pace himself—so that he *can* get his second wind!

Sherwood's Popeye, a descendant of Anderson's Champion Tonka. Owner, Matt White.

For, in an important sense, it is that curious phenomenon, the second wind, that makes possible the incredible feats of endurance our dogs are expected to perform, and *do* perform. It is certainly a curious phenomenon, and really quite wonderful when you think about it— the so-called second wind. That our dogs, or you or I for that matter, might be making our marathon run— and to our tired, striving bodies it seeming like forever before we can reach that desired point so far off in the distance. . . . And then, just when we're wondering how in the world we are ever going to make it, something clicks in! Where before we were tight and hurting, our muscles suddenly loosen up, our labored breathing eases and we breathe freely. Our step lightens, we are as light as air. It is as if there is more oxygen in our blood, indeed as if the very composition of our blood has changed, become charged with a vitality that comes from—where?

I'm sure I don't know. I'm neither a god nor a scientist, though some folks sometimes confuse the latter for the former. It's enough for me simply to glean the practical from my experiences.

Not pacing, going all out to an early exhaustion, cancels out the possibility of the second wind's properly settling in!

No such problem with Dusty. She

Riptide Pogo is a son of Hoover out of Tar. He, thus, has as immediate ancestors Grand Champion Hope, Grand Champion Barney and Grand Champion Hank.

Champion Spike is a son of Hammonds's Rufus.

trots along nicely beside my bike and is fairly loosened up when we reach a small park about a mile away. It's early morning and we have the park all to ourselves. It's a good safe place to let Dusty out of harness, for the park is all fenced in and no other pooch is going to sneak up on us.

As soon as she's loose she's circling round me, trying to catch a glimpse of the rolled-up bit of leather hide I have sticking out of my back pocket. I pull it out, hold it stretched between my hands, and she nails it!

What have we done so far? We've had the light trot up to the park, which simulates the walk before the match. And now immediately Dusty is going through the same motions as I expect she will in her match—except this time it's the hide she's tugging at and not her opponent's ear. And she's using jaw power, just as she will be in the hard-fought beginning of her match.

I keep it active—pulling, pushing, lifting Dusty's front paws off the ground, which simulates the other dog's rearing up. I do *not* send Dusty flying through the air while she hangs on. Not only is this unnecessary but foolish as well. Very nice, her slipping off and landing backward! A conditioned dog is hard to hurt, but why risk it?

"Say, pal, how come you had to forfeit?"

"Oh well, see, I threw my dog through the air...!"

If it's airborne that gives you a kick, get a canary!

As I hold the hide in one hand, I grab at Dusty's front legs with the other. She tucks her legs back so that

I cannot reach them, which is just what I want her to do. "Atta girl, tuck those legs!" And when she shakes, I say "Shake! Dusty—*shake* it!" I say it in a special voice, very excited, growling it even—whatever excites *her*! (Originally, I had to let *her* cue *me* when to say it. Later, after that sort of preparation, quite often she'd shake at *my* cue—when I told her to.)

After 20 minutes or so of this, *I've* had enough even if Dusty hasn't! So here we go down the road again,

even deep into Dusty's match, when I'll want her to have enough juice to turn it on if I ask her to. I might ask her to shake out a hold, or I might want to call her up if she's been down for a time.

We do five miles in this manner.

Now with Dusty there is always the option of parking the bike in some mesquite and *walking* her the next five miles. She's a puller and won't let up. If she were not a puller, I'd go on with the bike. There is precious

Band, a 32-pound son of Grand Champion Charlie. Owner, Stephanie Shreve.

down to the cattle guard, cross over it, and onto the dirt road which measures 2½ miles to the next cattle guard, one round trip between the guards being 5 miles' distance.

It's the occasional sight of a fleeing rabbit up ahead, or cattle in the distance—and my voice encouragement too—that sends Dusty on her wind sprints. I'll be wanting an occasional wind sprint out of Dusty even after the 20-mile mark. These wind sprints are, to my mind, the equivalent of those times,

little time or opportunity for "coasting" in a match, and so I don't want Dusty letting up too much during her workout. A lively trot is permissible, but that's coasting enough! An easy walk is as good as a dead stop! No good.

There is one, and one only, important exception to this rule of keeping the work steady through to the end of the workout and the desired distance. And that exception is that the workout must be *cut short* if you should determine that your

A six-month-old pup out of Heinzl's Raquel.

dog is "not right," which nine times out of ten means either *not rested enough* or perhaps that your dog's menu needs to be re-thought out. The spring in the step, especially in the hindquarters, is the giveaway, the indicator. There ought always to be a certain lightness of step, even after 20 or more miles of roadwork. Always, from the beginning to the end of the workout, there ought to be this spring in the step telling you that your dog has at least one more good wind spring in reserve, is still strong enough and enthusiastic enough. Naturally, your dog is not going to remain fresh through 25 miles of roadwork, but even so, some trace of that lightness of step will remain throughout, so long as your dog is right. Your dog ought never—I repeat, *never*—be permitted to reach

Henry's Ben. Owner, Gary Bouwkamp.

Heinzl's Sadie. Owner, Howard Heinzl.

that point where listlessness sets in, onset of a heavy weariness, hindquarters dragging. The best, the only wise thing for you to do at this point, is to turn around, walk your dog home, and give him five full days of rest.

You've got a good worker if your dog enjoys a variety of exercises. Most any exercise is helpful in some way, but only you can decide which exercises are most appropriate, will most benefit your dog matchwise. And only you can decide how these exercises are to be applied. As I've stressed again and again, everything that Dusty is doing in her workout somehow translates into some aspect of what she is actually to experience in her match. Again, variety is good, but the workout must continue on and not slacken below an acceptable point (barring exception mentioned above). Alternating the trotting and the wind sprints develops

endurance. Walking and pulling hard develops strength in a way that running cannot, as well as endurance.

So now that we're well into this Part Two, you see that my way of working a dog leaves far more leeway for improvisation than was perhaps apparent in Part One. Part One laid down the basic rule, the rationale I follow. But now you see that many variations on the theme are possible. Our workouts can be likened to an improvised solo in the jazz vein, the "taking off" which calls upon all the musician's musical creativity—and yet the same basic chord structure is never totally lost sight of!

These workouts are long ones, especially toward the end of the conditioning, and there is no time for a break once the workout has begun. If I *walk* Dusty as well as run her beside the bike, a workout might last between 4 to 6 hours. So many hours on the road can be quite tedious for a dog man. I own up to at times having become quite impatient with a dog, especially one that wasn't a good worker. I'd give a few harder tugs than I ought to have given, or I might string together the sort of pyrotechnic strain of verbal abuse only an East-Coast-born Italian can render. But these are things I would immediately regret. Even if it was a fool lump of a dog I was

of any dog I've ever seen. She'd earned the nickname "Beefy" for all the muscle there, and those big beefed-up hindquarters could launch her over any fence there ever was—especially if there was a cat on the other side! Hard to describe the workings of those hindquarters of hers, for I've never, before or since, seen a dog put together in quite that way. More than mere muscle development, I believe there was something rare, if not unique, in her

Walsh's Black Hole of Calcutta. Owners, Mike and Terry Walsh.

conditioning, it was my job to search out a way that worked. Firmness has its place in conditioning a dog. Losing one's temper does not!

So while you're out there, really *be* with your dog. Every individual dog is a study. Watch the way those legs work. Why is the way one dog is put together more efficient than the way some other dog is put together? When I was working Tuffy, I never ceased to be fascinated by the way her hindquarters worked when she was in a canter, that gait quicker than a trot but still short of a full run. She had the best hindquarters

very bone structure. And whatever it was, it was good—and it was *extremely* good! I raised a litter of eleven out of her, and not one of those pups inherited those wonderful hindquarters of hers. So many years since I've seen old Tuffy moving out, and yet I'll never forget the sight of her when she'd got her stride. With most dogs' hindquarters you notice a slight favoring of one side, a sort of "stepping off" on one side, the other less-favored side accepting the "push," a sort of give-and-receive response, slightly uneven. With Tuffy, both sides

Duchess, by Heinzl's Gringo out of Patrick's Miss Boomer. Owner, Sara Chapman.

Above left: Champion Little Cleo out of one of the best bulldog litters ever produced (Plumber's Soko ex Plumber's Cleo). Owner, Garry Hammonds. *Left:* S.&W. Champion Fox with Terry Williams and sons. *Above:* Brad McClure with McClure's Little Bonnie.

worked evenly and in a straight rotary fashion, like two pistons going in turn, perfect symmetry, perfect synchronization. It was a sight to see. And I don't know if I'll ever again see that in another dog!

I've gone on considerably about Tuffy, but, you see, the point is to *be* there with your dog. There is so much to see, so much to study, and hence so much to *miss*! I mean if rather than thinking about working my dog, I'd been thinking about nuzzling up to some movie starlet, I might not even have noticed that something special about Tuffy's hindquarters. Every subtlety, every nuance that you miss, you are that much less efficient in what you are trying to accomplish, and perhaps, in a deeper sense, that much poorer for it.

(Oh, that about the movie starlet, Hon—I was single at the time, remember. You can put the lamp down now, my own true love. I might be king of my castle, but I don't require crowning.)

So we've done our 25 or 30 miles with Dusty. We've let her follow her nose down the open road and we've followed along with her, shared her joy and excitement. And when, as the hours wore on and tedium would begin to set in, I serenaded us all by breaking into song. Several songs,

Champion Brock, a Staffordshire Bull Terrier in England.

Dollie's Brindle Tyrant.

actually, Sinatra tunes mostly, but one or two of Mozart's flute concerti, and Dusty loves a good bop vocal as well. (If you have *really* been along, dear reader, I wouldn't have been nearly so uninhibited. Of course an occasional steer would turn his head and give me the most curious look . . . pained. However, it is common knowledge what poor musical critics steers make, so I didn't let it bother me any.)

There is one last finishing touch we put on Dusty's workout. It's back to the park for 15 minutes more work on the hide. You know my rationale by now. Is it fairly obvious to you why we finish up with the hide? Think a moment, I'll wait. . . .

Good for you, those of you who have it!

The answer: We all know that in the pit the dogs tend to lose their bite as the match wears on. At this, our simulated finish of Dusty's "match," we want her biting hard, finishing strong. It's as simple as that.

This time was for Dusty, our last time down that long road together—mild, gentle-eyed, graceful, athletic, pretty little thing that she was—and the best little ear fighter I ever saw!

For you, Dusty!

Iron Jaws
Mabies Buddy, a
champion pit
dog who is also
an obedience
competition
winner. Owner,
W.E. Ritz.

PIT BULL HYSTERIA GENERATED BY UNFAVORABLE PUBLICITY

This is an article I did for the local San Diego evening paper, The Tribune, *during the height of the hysteria. (At least, I hope it was the height!) Into this short column I tried to squeeze the essence of what this book is all about.*

These are times of misery to those of us who are American Pit Bull Terrier devotees.

It may even be worse to me than with other owners, for I have written three books about the breed, and have written articles which assured people that the true nature of my favorite breed was extremely stable with people. They could be trusted beyond almost all other breeds not to bite, let alone attack, a human

This dog displays the red nose that was the "badge" of the Old Family Red Nose strain, but bona fide descendants of that strain are rare.

being.

The extremely bad publicity has generated a Pit Bull hysteria that inspires political demagogues to call for the banning of the breed.

The question is: Have I been misleading the public? Am I blinded by foolish devotion to an unworthy breed? If the answers are "no" to these and other questions that might properly be asked, then how do I square what I have said with all the news events recently reported, topped off with an Ann Landers column vilifying the breed?

First, I am not alone in my defense of the breed. The head of the Humane Society of the United States stated in a nationally televised interview that the problem is a people problem and not a Pit Bull problem. According to him, the annual number of canine-induced fatalities has stayed about the same. It is just that, in previous years, German Shepherds and Doberman Pinschers were being blamed. Now it is Pit Bulls. Apparently, the types of people that are causing such mischief with Pit Bulls formerly had other dogs with formidable characteristics.

Richard Avanzino, the head of an animal-welfare division in San Francisco, states that the only problem with Pit Bulls is that they are such fine dogs that they'll do anything to please their masters. Hence, if they have a criminal master, they can be trained to do criminal things. He emphasizes that is the only fault of the breed.

Richard Koehler, the dean of dog trainers and author of several classic books about dog training, has sent a letter to Ann Landers, letting her know that she is barking up the wrong tree in regard to the inherent viciousness of Pit Bulls toward humans. And I am not about to comment about a woman who was unable to hold her own marriage together, presuming to give advice on personal problems to letter writers, let alone on dogs about which she obviously is ignorant.

I have owned American Pit Bull Terriers for more than 40 years. In all that time, I never had one that would bite a person. That was because they were not so inclined. I had few that ever attacked other dogs. That was because I kept them confined and on leash when walking them, as is required by a San Diego ordinance for all dogs.

One of the times that a dog of mine attacked another dog was when I unleashed my 45-pound Pit Bull on a Great Dane that was mauling a 10-year-old boy in the Laguna Mountains. That was more than 10 years ago. If that boy still lives in San Diego, I want him to know that it was a Pit Bull that saved his life.

It is possible that more lives are saved each year by Pit Bulls than are taken by all dogs. The breed is used as a catch dog for rough stock on cattle ranches and pig farms. Ranchers have told me that they estimate that untold numbers of human lives could well have been lost if they had to go down into the rough terrain, trying to get a rope on some recalcitrant steer.

The Pit Bull has a disposition similar to the Labrador Retriever with humans. As with the Labrador breed, there are occasional aberrations from the norm. Unlike the Labrador, a people-mean Pit Bull—rare as it may be—will get nationwide publicity if it bites someone.

Because of the breed's history as a fighting dog, news stories regarding the misdeeds of a Pit Bull get more play and more reaction from the public than those of other breeds. There persists the misconception that a dog that would attack other dogs is bound to be vicious.

Some vicious-dog ordinances define a dog as vicious if it attacks domestic animals. This is sheer folly, and many breed show standards—the Boxer's, to name one—specify that aggression toward other canines is not to be considered viciousness.

The point is that the majority of American Pit Bull Terriers have a strong urge to fight other dogs. But the individual dogs that will attack people are so rare that breeders have been known to obtain other breeds to guard their kennels.

Unfortunately, Pit Bulls have become popular—especially with the macho groups, the very people who are most likely to keep a vicious Pit Bull.

Besides the problem of the kooks to which the breed has such

Kitty and Dharma watch Dharma's bodyguard jump for stick.

overwhelming appeal, there is the problem of the name that is used so much, Pit Bull. It is an imprecise term, not really used by breed enthusiasts, as it applies to several other breeds, including the Bull Terrier and American Staffordshire Terrier, and is always used to refer to any dog with an appearance along those lines. Thus, more attacks are attributed to the American Pit Bull Terrier breed than it actually commits.

Because of the fact that the breed is so popular and the type of culling out of any people-mean dogs is not taking place now in the breeding programs of many backyard breeders, there are probably more vicious Pit Bulls now than ever before. But they are still in the distinct minority—an absolute aberration of the breed. So despite what appears in the news, the American Pit Bull Terrier breed is still of stable temperament, and it is a unique dog.

Present law holds dog owners strictly accountable for the actions of their charges. A man in Florida is serving time in custody for manslaughter because of the actions of his Pit Bull. Two people in this state face a similar fate. That fact should demonstrate that no new law is needed and should give pause to those who would keep a people-mean Pit Bull.

Above: **Blue Eyed Lady. Owner, Jude Levasseur.** *Opposite:* **Champion Sodbuster, also known as "Peanut," is a very game pit dog. It was said to pack a lunch if he was going up against a tough opponent, as you were going to be there for a while.**

The Pit and the Pendulum

"Hope, deceitful as it is, serves at least to lead us to the end of life along an agreeable road."
La Rochefoucauld

As I write this final chapter, the American Pit Bull Terrier breed is under even heavier fire than ever. There are three reasons for the intensification of the attacks against the breed. One is that a two-year-old youngster was recently killed in northern California by an American Pit Bull Terrier. Then, only a few days later, a television crew filmed an attack of a Bulldog on an animal control officer. That attack made my heart beat fast in horror, and yet, the dog was not nearly as intense and deadly as a game dog would have been. (Luckily, however, game dogs seem not to be people-mean.)

Finally, there has been a recognition that a predominant number of the fatal attacks in the last three years have been committed by Pit Bulls.

It is interesting to note that though the fatal attacks in the last few years have been primarily by Pit Bulls, there are not more fatal attacks than there were ten or fifteen years ago. It was just that back then the attacks were made by a variety of different breeds. What that tells me is that the same types of people that once owned the other dogs have all become convinced that the APBT is the "toughest" dog, and they have all gravitated to it.

The Welshman Angel.

Among such people, responsible dog ownership is not stressed or, perhaps, even given momentary thought. In my opinion, they are, generally speaking, either the macho group or the ghetto types that really don't understand dogs in general, let alone the Bulldog. Of course, the general population doesn't really understand dogs either, but most of them make an effort to learn about a breed of dog when they purchase an individual of that particular breed.

The problem then is one of overpopularity of the breed, which results (in any breed) in non-selective breeding by ignorant breeders, who then put the pups up for sale in the local paper for a relatively low price. Then, since the breeder really knows nothing, the buyer either gets very little information, or worse yet, misinformation about how to take care of his dog and what to expect.

Now, Pit Bulls are still way down in the bite statistics. The problem is that they figure prominently in the fatal attack statistics. I wrote many years ago that a Bulldog was "a thousand times less likely to attack than another breed," but if he did "he would be a thousand times more dangerous." Thus, it has come to pass that we have a certain number of Bulldogs that will attack humans. This has come about because of the extreme popularity of the breed and the non-selective breeding resulting therefrom.

Furthermore, there is the problem of the media's fascination for the breed and a tendency for it to present any stories about it in a sensationalized manner. The worse the paper, the more irresponsible and undisciplined is the sensationalism. However, even respected papers, magazines, and television shows have, to some degree, followed the same path.

Since I am the author of several books on the American Pit Bull Terrier, I receive calls from all the major newspapers and magazines, as well as offers to appear on various talk show forums. I have given rather freely of my time in the usually vain hope that I can add a semblance of perspective to the situation. Some articles which appeared in print, rare as they may be, have turned out terrific. Most have been veritable hatchet jobs on the breed and its owners, apparently pandering to the public's appetite for the sensational and even the macabre.

As an illustration of how these things work, let me pursue one publication only and how it approached the story. The magazine is *Sports Illustrated*, and it so happens that story appeared recently. Here is how I first heard about it and what happened subsequently.

Apparently, Hector Cazarez, the head of the animal control center in San Diego, had been contacted by the magazine; at least, he was the first person who told me that *Sports Illustrated* was going to do a story on the breed. My wife made a facetious comment that at least now they had the right magazine; however, both of us were unhappy to hear that a story was to be done, as bitter experience had taught us that such stories were usually sensationalistic and completely misrepresentative of the American Pit Bull Terrier breed.

A few days later, I received a call from Ed Swift, the man who was writing the piece. As usual, I was

An English canine, double-bred Hagler bitch, being shown in a conformation contest.

289

cooperative, and I could only hope for the best. He had read my first book, he told me; however, nearly all writers tell me that they have read one or more of my books. Unfortunately, subsequent conversation usually indicates that they have done no such thing. At the most they have perused it, perhaps looking at the photographs and drawings. Either that or they have very poor retention. To some degree, Swift seemed to me to have certainly not read the book carefully, but he had at least done more than look at the pictures.

After a long interview by phone, Swift thanked me for my cooperation. At that point, I asked him if he covered the San Diego sports teams, too. Upon being told that he did indeed, including the hapless Padres, I facetiously said, "Well, you know what I have had to put up with in the case of the Padres and the Chargers, so the Pit Bull hysteria is really adding to the poor status of my mental health. So please be kind in the article."

Actually, the way the article was written was not too bad when compared with other articles done by even respected magazines such as *Time* and *Newsweek*. It was primarily the picture display that was used to fuel the hysteria. For example, on the cover was a snarling Pit Bull and big headlines above it that exhorted

Medders' Tiger Jack is sired by Apache Red Ty and is of predominantly Old Family Red Nose breeding.

Riptide Bandit reaching up for the ball stuck in the fence.

"Beware this Dog!" It would be interesting to know how they got the dog on the cover to bare his teeth as shown, for it is not the general nature of the breed to do so. Ironically, I had given even more generously of my time for the photo display than for the interview. One of the managers from *Sports Illustrated* called and asked if they could send a photography team out to my place and take pictures of my dogs. I acquiesced and a team of two men came out to my place and took many pictures of my dogs.

They took pictures of Hoover opening the gate. They took pictures of me with each of my dogs. They took pictures of Hoover and Isaac together. And they took pictures of Hoover and Isaac playing ball on the hill in back of my place. Hundreds of pictures were taken, and after the session, which lasted at least three hours, the two men were talking together. One of them explained, "We were just saying that these dogs are ten times as cooperative as most professional athletes and probably smarter, too!"

The only picture taken at my place that appeared in the article was one of Hoover jumping up at the gate of a fenced yard. (Actually, he was jumping up and down in excitement of my holding a ball. But the camera froze him, so that it might seem as though he was coming over.) Anyway, that picture alone was run with the caption "A fenced yard can't keep Stratton's Hoover in." The clear inference was that Hoover was able to get out of a fenced area and would be dangerous if he were at large. You really have to know Hoover and the situation to understand just how ludicrous that caption was.

Some pictures were rerun from an article that appeared in *Geo*'s article on dogfighting which had appeared many years ago, and I had criticized it in the *American Pit Bull Terrier Gazette* as extremely misleading and downright false. Yet, Swift referred to the "classic" article by *Geo*, and he derived much of his erroneous information from that. He managed to get other misinformation from, among others, a San Diego judge who said, "A Pit Bull is the closest thing to a wild animal as any domestic pet." One has to know a little about wild animals and Pit Bulls to appreciate just how asinine such a statement is. It is a common misconception that wild animals are

Below: Dixieland Diamond Girl as a pup. Owner, Sara Chapman. *Opposite:* Riptide Bandit having reached the ball eight feet off the ground.

vicious. Of course, many will bite in self-defense, but then they immediately try to escape. One of the problems here is that the public is inclined to confuse predation with aggression. It is quite different in wild animals. With predation, the predator selects the easiest prey available and dispatches it as quickly as possible with no more malice toward the prey than we would have toward a cherry pie! In

been ever thus. Those who make disparaging comments about the breed are precisely those people who have, to put it charitably, very limited knowledge on the subject. And yet everyone has an opinion about the Pit Bull, and they seem to be blissfully unaware that their opinion is not really theirs at all. It has been conditioned in them, Pavlovian style, by the media.

The main problem with the breed

Left: **Pups down from Snooty, owned by Matt White.**

Opposite: **Jeff Burke with Brewer's Outlaw, also a son of Snooty.**

aggressive behavior, the animals usually rely on threat display and only actually fight if the threat display is not sufficient—and such cases are rare. There is good reason for such a state of affairs, as an injured wild animal is one that is at great disadvantage in competing and surviving in the wild.

The point is that one of the weaknesses of the article was that people who were by no means expert in their knowledge of the Pit Bull were quoted on the same level as those who had some idea of what they were talking about. Unfortunately, the ignorant ones were the source of the deprecatory comments. To my perception, it has

is that it has become popular, and aberrational individuals are in the hands of irresponsible people. However, the media, while not creating the core of the problem, has certainly made it worse by their almost invariable sensationalistic coverage of it. The sad thing is that the absolutely insane publicity has resulted in many people being afraid of their own dogs. And these are people with dogs that have been models of good behavior for many years. Yet the people fear that the dogs will turn on them, as that is what they have been led to believe by quotes in the news. For example, frequently the statement is made that a Pit Bull is a time bomb waiting

to go off. The only way such a statement has any validity is in the case of a Bulldog's behavior with other dogs. Any time over a year of age, a Bulldog can develop a strong urge to fight other dogs (and sometimes other animals as well). Usually, this is with strange dogs, though, and I have known many a son of a line of champion pit dogs that lived in harmony with a prior family pet. Two Bulldogs together is a little more tricky situation, and I always recommend that such dogs not be left unsupervised together.

One of the authorities that the news writers turn to are the various animal welfare heads in various cities. Now the humane groups are in a tricky situation. For they have always been able to solicit many financial contributions by taking the offensive against dogfighting. As a group, they have parroted each other for over a decade now in regard to various alleged pit-dog atrocities, such as "blooding" pit dogs with pigeon blood, training the dogs with the use of kittens, and amputating the dogs' front legs so that they are able to get under the opponent and reach his belly! Such constant publicity about these inane practices has given young street toughs ideas that they may never have had otherwise. In effect, humane organizations, because of the publicity they put out, have caused inhumane acts.

Perhaps it should be pointed out that a common fiction is that tasting blood makes a Bulldog more savage. Here again, we have the confusion of aggression (or fighting) with predation. Pouring blood over a Bulldog is not likely to make him more inclined to fight than applying catsup or water, for that matter. The

Tucker and Kitty the Bulldog.

Ironman's Pee Wee, a descendant of Peterbilt and Grand Champion Hank. Owner, Jeff Fontenot.

kitten story is an outgrowth of the common misconception that a fighting dog is by nature vicious or must be made that way. Presumably, teasing him with kittens and allowing him to kill them is supposed to make him a more effective fighting dog or, at the very least, make him more vicious or aggressive. Such is not the case, and many extremely game pit dogs have no inclination to kill kittens anyway. I told the *Sports Illustrated* about all this, but he chose to follow the ravings of those who have promulgated all these ridiculous stories.

Above: Belker, an APBT, beat Champion Gnasher in a pit contest. *Below:* Troy's Terror is a 35-pound daughter of Boomer.

Pat Graham with her dog Rhino in England.

Riff-Raff, a son of Little Boots, places at a show.

When it comes right down to it, the humane groups don't really know much about pit dogs. But they always suspect the very worst and any evidence they might receive is always interpreted in that mind-set. Whatever they put out to reporters or in their own publications is always sensationalized and, of course, is in no way objective. Thus any story, no matter how farfetched, is reported as fact, usually with no apparent attempt at confirmation. It is easy to see why they are so willing to believe anything they hear, as they conceive of dogfighting as the ultimate in premeditated cruelty. People capable of such acts are, in their mind, capable of anything, so

why should there be cause for doubt. A favorite quotation of mine (and I can't remember who said it) is "Skepticism is the chastity of the intellect." To me that is a profound statement and one that human agents would do well to heed when receiving stories of pit dogs.

I, myself, am not without regard for humane agents, as I care about animals, and I don't want to see them mistreated. Besides, some humane persons have had the good sense to think that maybe I had something to teach them. And they have submitted proposed laws for my perusal and suggestions. Further, many have demonstrated that they like the breed. These are usually people who have had a chance to experience the good nature and intelligence of these dogs.

Other humane agents seem to have an obvious hatred for the breed, and I think that is primarily because they have not come to know it and, secondarily, a dog that is a danger to other dogs is more odious to maudlin dog lovers than one that is a danger to humans. Still, though, some humane agents (notice how I'm being good and not employing my term, "humaniac"!) may beat the drums for

surely the next hysteria will target another breed.

I have railed against the idea of the Pit Bull being a vicious dog because I know what a prevarication that is. And I am all too aware of just what a mockery of justice it would be to have this most stable of breeds outlawed. Irony of ironies, at the very time that there is such a hue and cry against the Pit Bull as though he was some sort of Frankenstein monster, with villagers out after him with torches in their hands, other countries are importing

Riptide Beauty is a good weight puller.

the abolition of dogfighting and even berate the dogs, they dare not suggest that there should be laws banning the breed. Such suggestions are usually on the part of other zealots who have been caught up in the hysteria. The reason humaniacs (oops!) who might want the breed banned would never suggest it is that the contributors to their organizations are largely purebred dog breeders. Such people have the sagacity to realize that once one breed is banned, the door is open to ban others. If the Pit Bull is banned,

American dogs. What we have denounced in America is being hailed abroad.

Although I don't like people-mean dogs, I challenge anyone's attempt to take away protection dogs. In this age of unbridled crime, people have a right to feel secure in their homes by being allowed a personal protection dog. But please, let's not have it be a Bulldog. First of all, even in these days, most Bulldogs are not good watch dogs. They don't bark much, and they like people. However, if you do get a people-

Shebest's Rosie making her presence known.

mean Bulldog, one that attacks a stranger as it would another dog, you have a truly dangerous animal on your hands. Because of his intensity and formidability, he would be entirely capable of killing a full-grown man. After all, these were dogs that battled lions at one time and are still used for taming wild boar and recalcitrant steers. Most of the attacks that have occurred have been by Pit-Bull mixes, part Staf or part German Shepherd or some other breed. Those that have been purebred were far removed from pit stock. And I think most of the attacks were half-hearted. As I mentioned earlier, we did not see the full brunt of what a Pit Bull is capable of doing in those telecasts of the attack on the animal control officer. No serious Pit Bull could be beaten off by a little white pole, as happened in that incident. No doubt the dog was not well bred, but he was probably encouraged to be protective.

There are certain themes that run through all this publicity that are mildly irritating to me because they are just plain wrong. One is the habit of constantly referring to the Pit Bull as a "species." Well, no breed of dog is a species. They are varieties of a species. It is for that reason that I capitalize the names of dog breeds—contrary to the habit of journalists. The names are proper nouns because they are the names of varieties. Another misstatement is that the viciousness that has surfaced in some Pit Bulls is due to inbreeding. That is just not so. Inbreeding is a valuable tool that is used in all selective breeding of all varieties of species. It is not desirable in wild animals, or

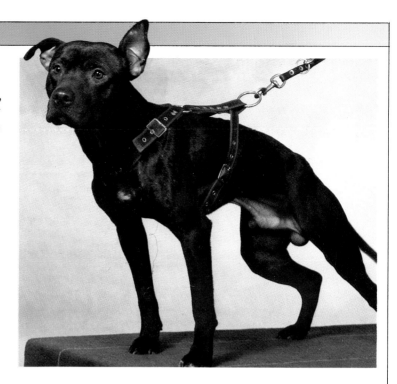

U and S's Tater, photographed a day before he won a pit contest.

humans, because diversity of the gene pool is desirable so that there will be adaptability to the environment. Simply put, what inbreeding does is reduce the variation within a gene pool, and doesn't in itself produce unstable temperament or other undesirable effects. An example of extreme inbreeding in dogs is in guide dogs for the blind!

Emmerts's Tugger participating in a weight-pull contest.

A tactic that is often used both in articles and various television programs is to call upon people who have been attacked by Pit Bulls or have witnessed such an attack. It is difficult to talk to such people, as anyone with human feelings is going to have extreme sympathy and compassion for anyone who has suffered such a tragedy. However, it should be pointed out that the position of such people would be that of an individual who was injured or had a family member killed by an automobile—and that is their only experience with the vehicles. The analogy is not entirely well taken (but I can't think of a better one), for while all automobiles are potentially dangerous, most Pit Bulls are not. Nevertheless, being hit by an auto doesn't make one an authority on those vehicles, and having Pit Bull victims on television shows or consulted is sheer sensationalism.

At this time, new laws are being proposed in countless municipalities. Some have already taken effect. When just one municipality, Hollywood, Florida, passed a law that singled out the Pit Bull for special treatment, a national campaign was mounted to get the ordinance removed. It was declared to be unconstitutional. The cynical intent of today's demagogues is to inundate the country with laws or ordinances so that there will not be the funds for a successful challenge. But, even if that strategy works, the

such a law.

Personally, I see no reason for new laws at all. There is no new problem. There have always been about twelve fatalities a year from dogs. And they have been dogs of all breeds including once, long ago, three Pekingese mauling a youth. What do we do? Outlaw all dogs? Owners are now strictly accountable for the actions of their dogs. People whose dogs have attacked and killed

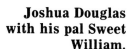

Joshua Douglas with his pal Sweet William.

ordinances will be unsuccessful and unenforceable. Such laws merely tend to make the citizenry contemptuous of laws in general.

So desperate are Pit Bull devotees that they are willing to embrace any law as long as it is not breed specific, as long as it doesn't single out Pit Bulls for special treatment— from an outright ban to requiring special quarters and insurance. I, however, am unwilling to accept any law that describes a vicious dog as one that shows a propensity for attacking domestic animals. Since most Pit Bulls will attack other dogs, they are automatically singled out in

are not infrequently prosecuted for manslaughter. A man in Georgia was sentenced to five years in custody for the actions of his dogs. Nor is this a new phenomenon. I recall some forty years ago when a Florida man was sentenced to even a longer time in prison because a pack of his dogs killed a woman.

Of course, it doesn't matter all that much what I think. Most of us are going to be living under new vicious dog legislation anyway. We already do in San Diego, but it is a quite reasonable ordinance when compared with the laws passed in other municipalities. If we have to have new laws, I would just as soon it be the death penalty if your dog kills someone not in the act of committing a crime. I wouldn't worry. People with guard dogs should take precautions to make sure innocent persons are not injured. As for me, I haven't ever had a Bulldog that would hurt anyone intentionally. I have never had a dog bite anyone, and I could live with the possibility that I would be in deep trouble if one of them did attack a person. Because it just isn't going to happen.

These are uncertain times for the Bulldog devotee, times of frustration and downright misery. But it is a time of challenge, too. I have always maintained that not just anyone should own a Bulldog. Those of us who have the perseverance to stick by the dogs will keep them. Others, hopefully, will drop them. I can hardly wait for a time that the Bulldog is no longer so popular. It may be a long time coming, but there is a pendulum effect in the popularity of all breeds. There is that same effect with hysterias, too. They may seem to last forever, but they will inevitably die down. In the end, we will prevail.

Already there have been some sign that cooler heads are providing a little perspective to the situation. Newspapers have run editorials pointing out that there is no need for

Perry's Champion Big Mac, a son of Champion Little Boots out of a daughter of Grand Champion Hank.

Left: Double D's Harley D., 44 pounds chainweight. *Below:* Duran's Bomber, a pit winner. Owner, Carl Clark.

new laws, and that the Pit Bull situation is being blown out of proportion. Andy Rooney, known mainly for his rather silly commentary addendum to the "Sixty Minutes" television program is actually a skillful and profound syndicated writer. And he has recently written a column defending the Pit Bull, artfully putting the whole media mess into perspective. Then, too, comedian David Steinberg talked on the Carson show about how the whole Pit Bull scare is a media event. I always suspected that comics were smarter than politicians—but, unfortunately, politicians are often funnier than comedians!

In the meantime, let's try to be the most responsible and educated of dog owners. Learn all you can about your breed. Learn about other breeds, too—it will make you appreciate Bulldogs all the more. Study about wolves and learn something about ethology (the study of animal behavior). If you become interested in biology, as I am, you will become aware that the humane agents are really barking up the wrong tree. For the real animal cruelty in the world is that we are crowding out all the other species at the alarming rate of over one a day.

For now, enjoy your Bulldogs. Let the hysteria run its course. Remain calm. Don't act like some nut in defense of your dogs. Remember, we are the reasonable ones. Look to your Bulldog. There is much that humankind can learn from this most remarkable animal. He is very likely the only example of true courage in the entire world. We humans can't even approximate his trait which even his enemies have difficulty demeaning. But we can take inspiration from such a noble animal. He has persevered in the most difficult of situations and somehow still maintains a certain charisma and dignity. His courage, gameness, and stark warrior spirit have seen him through difficult times before. Is it too much to ask that his human companions, who so admire him, show at least a little of those same traits? If we do, we will once again allow the American Pit Bull Terrier not only to continue, but to prevail.

Colby's Lotus, bred and owned by Louis Colby, is the dam of many good dogs throughout the United States.

Annotated Bibliography

I am including books here that I think will be of interest to the serious dog fancier, as well as periodicals of interest to the student of the breed. I have taken the liberty to include under organizations a couple of outfits that readers who are as concerned as I am about the extinction of animals may wish to join.*

BOOKS

Armitage, George C. *Thirty Years with Fighting Dogs*. Washington, D.C.: Privately published, 1936.

This book is mainly of historical interest, but it provides a look into the rather hoody element of dogfighting that existed in Armitage's time and locality.

Barrie, Anmarie, Esq. *Dogs and the Law*. 211 West Sylvania, Neptune City, New Jersey: T.F.H. Publications, Inc., 1989.

An easy-to-read reference handbook on canines and the American legal system. This animal-author/attorney presents the pit bull case and other current owner concerns.

Brown, Wayne D. *History of the Pit Bull Terrier*. Dallas, Texas: Privately published, 1979.

Brown has made a serious attempt to trace the different strains of Bulldogs back to their origins in England and Ireland, apparently using various periodicals for sources. The book contains pictures and a vast quantity of pedigrees.

Colby, Joseph L. *The American Pit Bull Terrier*. Sacramento, California: Privately published, 1936.

Written by one of John P. Colby's sons, this little book contains many old photographs of dogs from the Colby line and gives accounts of matches of several dogs. It contains articles by other dog men too, including an article by the founder of the United Kennel Club.

Davis, Henry P., editor. *The New Dog Encyclopedia*. New York: Galahad Books, 1970.

This book gives information on the American Kennel Club show breeds and their show standards; but, unlike other so-called "complete" dog books, it does not pretend that there are no other breeds outside that body's recognition. In fact, it gives information on such things as tree hounds and Border Collies. It also gives a history of the United Kennel Club and the American Field registry. It also has sections on field trials of various types (i.e., pointing dogs, retrievers, hounds, water races, and herding dog trials), sections on diseases and parasites, and information on training.

Denlinger, Milo G. *The Complete Pit Bull or Staffordshire Terrier*. Washington, D.C.: Denlingers, 1948.

This book consists of a compilation of articles derived from old *Bloodlines* magazines, from old books on the Staffordshire Bull Terrier, and from works on the American Staffordshire Terrier, as well as other sources. It can be confusing to beginners, but it contains many old photographs, articles on matches (especially the old classic ones), and historically significant old woodcuts and paintings. Despite its faults, it is a quality book, excellently bound with good paper and high-quality photographs. It is now a collector's item, and the last price list I saw carried it at a couple hundred dollars for a single copy! (now it's probably much more).

De Prisco, Andrew and James B. Johnson. *The Mini-Atlas of Dog Breeds*. 211 West Sylvania, Neptune City, New Jersey: T.F.H. Publications, Inc., 1990.

Authors present over 400 breeds of dog in an entertaining but straightforward way. Each breed is illustrated and described according to its origin, body type, character and registry. A handbook to be reckoned with and a must-have for all dog lovers.

Eberhard, Ernest. *The New Complete Bull Terrier*. New York: Howell Book House, Inc., 1971.

This is a typical breed book, but it is of good quality, especially for those who want to learn about a breed that is often confused with ours.

Ehrlich, Paul and Anne. *Extinction: The Causes and Consequences of the Disappearance of Species*. New York: Random House, 1981.

This is not directly about Bulldogs, but it deals with the alarming extinction of other species of which I've written in this work. The book spells out for the reader in detail the cause and consequences of these extinctions, and I urge all intelligent

people to read it.

Fox, Richard K. *The Dog Pit*. New York: Police Gazette Publishers, *circa* 1910.

This book was written by the editor of the *Police Gazette* magazine. To view this book in perspective, it is important for the reader to know that the *Police Gazette* was a combination *National Enquirer–Playboy–Sports Illustrated* of its times. Actually, I can't think of a comparable publication now. It covered many illegal sports of that time, including boxing, wrestling, cockfighting, and dogfighting. This book should by no means be considered an authoritative breed book—it is full of much hogwash. The stories about fights between Bulldogs and bobcats and monkeys and so on are probably all fabrications. Nonetheless, it is an interesting book and contains drawings of such famous old dogs as "Cincinnati Paddy" and "Crib." It also contains the *Police Gazette* rules for a pit contest.

Glass, Eugene. *The Sporting Bull Terrier*. Battle Creek, Michigan: Privately published, 1910.

Mr. Glass was the editor of a pit dog magazine of the time called the *Dog Fancier*. His book contains rules, a keep, instructions for building a kennel, and information on the use of training devices. Amazing is the tremendous amount of misinformation that is contained in the book. Two examples will suffice. For the springpole, it is suggested that a coonskin be used as the part for the dog to grasp and hang from. Now, any dog man who has ever tried a coon hide for this purpose knows that it very quickly disintegrates. The author also talks about the white show Bull Terrier as though it were just a fancy show version of the

Pit Bulldog and "just as game." Ridiculous on both counts!

Gonick, Larry and Mark Wheelis. *The Cartoon Guide to Genetics.* New York: Barnes and Noble Books, 1983.

This is an excellent manner for the layman to learn the history of some of our genetic knowledge. The book is extremely informative and incredibly funny—without distorting the information a bit! It may take someone who already has a knowledge of the history of genetic research to appreciate just how funny this book is.

Hall, Bobby. *Bullyson and His Sons.* Houston, Texas: Walsworth Press Company, 1986.

This work is like a modern-day Armitage book, but it is probably of more interest to readers because it deals with more modern dogs. It is a book that will be mainly of interest to fanciers who are quite knowledgeable about the dogs already.

Jones, Mitchell. *The Dogs of Capitalism.* Austin, Texas: 21st Century Logic, 1988.

Although not a typical dog book in any sense, this book has to be recognized as a serious contribution to American Pit Bull Terrier lore and history. The bizarre title is from the author's interpretation of history and current events in the light of the philosophy of objectivism.

Maffie, Fredric. *The Life of Humbug.* New York: Manor Books, Inc., 1979.

This is a fiction book, but it is written by a knowledgeable dog man and contains much information on pit dogs. It is presently out of print, so copies that are found will likely command a high price.

_____. *Red Tina (A Fighting Dog).* Winona, Minnesota: Apollo Books, 1985.

Again, a fiction book, but one by a master writer and a real authority on the dogs. In spite of its subject, it is quite likely to end up in anthologies of best dog stories.

Matz, K.S. *The Pit Bull, Fact and Fable.* Sacramento, California: DeMortmain Books, 1984.

The author of this book has gone to old public writings and reprinted many old pictures and references which should be extremely valuable to the student of the breed.

Meeks, Jack. *Memoirs of the Pit.* Starke, Florida: Privately published by Pete Sparks, 1974.

Although this book was published in 1974, the manuscript was actually compiled in the mid-1930s, so it is of interest historically.

Nicholas, Anna Katherine. *The Staffordshire Terriers: The American Staffordshire Terrier and the Staffordshire Bull Terrier.* 211 West Sylvania, Neptune City, New Jersey: T.F.H. Publications, Inc., 1990.

Presents the Staffordshire breeds in terms of performances in AKC conformation and obedience trials. Many such "champions" illustrated. Not my kind of book, but well done for what it is.

Onstott, Kyle. *The New Art of Breeding Better Dogs.* New York: Howell Book House, Inc., 1973.

This is a very thorough treatise on the subject. It puts the bugaboos of inbreeding to rest.

Pfaffenberger, Clarence. *The New Knowledge of Dog Behavior.* New

York: Howell Book House, Inc., 1963.

This easy-to-read book gives fairly technical knowledge about dogs in a very palatable manner. It dispels much nonsense about dog behavior and inbreeding. It deals with the training of dogs for various tasks but primarily for the training and selective breeding of guide dogs for the blind.

Pierce, Rev. Thomas. *The Dog.* London: Cassel and Co., 1872.

Pierce wrote under the name of Idestone, as it was the style of the day to use a *nom de plume*, and he perpetuated many wild tales about dog activities. There is no way to check them now, of course, and no one bothered to check them during his era. He was a controversial and promotion-minded figure of his times. Any would-be cynologist should be familiar with these types of writings, for they influenced those who came later.

Scott, John Paul and John L. Fuller. *The Genetic Basis of Dog Behavior.* Chicago: University of Chicago Press, 1965.

This is one of the classic studies of inheritance of behavioral traits. The writing is scientific but readable and an absolute must for the amateur cynologist.

Semencic, Dr. Carl, *The World of Fighting Dogs.* 211 West Sylvania, Neptune City, New Jersey: T.F.H. Publications, Inc., 1984.

Dr. Semencic has put together a good overview of the various fighting breeds utilized throughout the world. He lets it be known that the American Pit Bull Terrier is the best of the lot, but he spends a lot of time on the other breeds, too.

_____. *Pit Bulls and Other Man-Stopping Guard Dogs.* 211 West Sylvania, Neptune City, New Jersey: T.F.H. Publications, Inc.

A colorful and expert survey of over 20 tough and able canines—of course Pit Bulls top the list (and make the title!). This book introduces and evaluates many exciting, up-and-coming protectors, including the Tosa, Dogue de Bordeaux, Canary Dog, and Fila Brasileiro, for starters.

Smith, Lt. Col. Charles Hamilton. *Dogs.* Edinburgh: np, 1840.

One of the first and one of the best treatises on dogs in the English language, this book should be of interest to the historian and cynologist. This is a book that the legitimate dog expert should read.

Walsh, Dr. J.H. *Dogs of the British Islands.* London: Horace Cox, 1867.

Walsh wrote under the *nom de plume* Stonehenge. This was probably the most influential dog book of its time. Again, this is a book that the legitimate dog expert must read.

Whitney, Dr. Leon F. *Dog Psychology, The Basis of Dog Training.* New York: Howell Book House, Inc., 1972.

I always recommend this book for those who are interested in training their dogs for any purpose whatsoever. This is a method of training that is based on the firm bedrock of scientific research, rather than on the intransigent opinions of some dog trainer. It is also recommended for those who would be better to understand their dogs.

_____. *Feeding Our Dogs.* New York: D. Van Nostrand, 1949.

Dr. Whitney was a veterinarian who

pioneered research in dog nutrition and many other areas, too, including distemper. If I were limited to suggesting just one author for reading, it would be Whitney. His writing style is direct, and the information he dispenses is immense.

Wilcox, Dr. Bonnie and Chris Walkowicz. *The Atlas of Dog Breeds of the World.* 211 West Sylvania, Neptune City, New Jersey: T.F.H. Publications, Inc., 1989.

Veterinarian Wilcox and well-known writer Walkowicz present intelligent and readable information on over 420 breeds of dog, essentially covering every breed recognized in the world today. It is fully illustrated and will remain a permanent source of reference for the dog world. Truly no book like it!

Youatt, William and E.J. Lewis. *The Dog.* New York: Levitt and Allen, 1846.

This is an American edition of a book that was originally published in London by Youatt in 1845. All editions of this work are rare and hard to find, so the reader may have to resort to a library search service and obtain it on either photocopies or microfilm.

Young, Stanley Paul. *The Clever Coyote.* Caldwell, Idaho: Caxton Printers, 1946.

———. *The Wolf in North American History.* Caldwell, Idaho: Caxton Printers, 1946.

———. *The Wolves of North America.* Caldwell, Idaho: Caxton Printers, 1950.

Stanley Paul Young was a real authority on wolves and coyotes, and he writes in a palatable manner. We learn about our domestic dogs by studying the wild ones, especially the wolf—but the coyote is extremely close to our dogs, too.

*Editor's note: Even Mr. Stratton is too modest to recommend books of his own authorship. His first three volumes on the Pit Bull Terrier are indispensable and have been unanimously hailed and well received by critics and readers alike. They are all available from the publisher.

This is the American Pit Bull Terrier, 1976.

The Book of the American Pit Bull Terrier, 1981.

The World of the American Pit Bull Terrier, 1983.

PERIODICALS

American Pit Bull Terrier Gazette. American Dog Breeders' Association, Box 1771, Salt Lake City, Utah 84110.

This periodical contains articles on all aspects of the American Pit Bull Terrier, and advertisements feature all the needs of the APBT devotee, including breaking sticks, treadmills, and harnesses. Featuring many fine articles, this magazine is pretty much the flagship of the breed now.

Animal Behavior. Bailliere Tendall, 7 & 8 Henrietta Street, Covent Garden, London WC2E-8QE.

This is a highly respected journal with technical articles on behavior of all animal species for those who want to become truly knowledgeable about dogs and species in general.

Coonhound Bloodlines. United Kennel Club, 100 East Kilgore Road, Kalamazoo, Michigan 49001-5597

The coonhounds are the bulwark of the UKC now, with many field trials and conformation shows being much larger than the AKC dog shows or field trials.

Bloodlines Journal. United Kennel Club, 100 East Kilgore Road, Kalamazoo, Michigan 49001-5597

This magazine carries a section on American Pit Bull Terriers.

Dog World. Judy-Berner Publishing Co., 469 Ohio Street, Chicago, Illinois.

Mainly concerned with show dogs, it occasionally publishes articles on show breeds with histories (dating back to the pharaohs!) that smack more of a lively imagination than scientific research. It usually contains some articles of general interest.

Pit Dog Report. P.O. Box 33509, Houston, Texas.
American periodical on Bulldogs.

Sporting Dog Journal. P.O. Box 476, Jefferson, Georgia.

Although not the oldest, this has been a very steady publication, always coming out just like clockwork. While intended for the pit dog man, non-sponsored inquiries will be considered.

ORGANIZATIONS

American Dog Breeders' Association, Box 1771, Salt Lake City, Utah 84110

This is a registry of the American Pit Bull Terrier and publisher of the *American Pit Bull Terrier Gazette*. It also sponsors weight pulls and dog shows for the breed.

American Dog Owners' Association, 1920 Route 9, Castleton, New York 12033

This is a coalition of dog owners of all breeds, and it has been in the forefront of the fight against breed-specific laws.

Endangered Breed Association

This organization has been involved in helping supply funds to individuals or groups who are being harassed simply because of their Bulldogs.

Negative Population Growth, 16 East 42nd Street, New York, New York 10164-9990

For those who share my alarm about the extermination of species, I am supplying the name and address of this organization which is giving its best efforts to address the cause of the extinctions.

United Kennel Club, 100 East Kilgore Road, Kalamazoo, Michigan 49001-5597

This is another registry for the American Pit Bull Terrier and is publisher of *Bloodlines* Journals. It also sponsors conformation shows for the breed.

Zero Population Growth, 1601 Connecticut Avenue, Washington, DC 20009

The purpose for including this organization is the same as that for including NPG above.

Index